THE NEW COLLEGE FINANCIAL AID SYSTEM

Making It Work For You

BY DAVID JAFFE

COUNCIL OAK BOOKS • TULSA

Council Oak Books
Tulsa, Oklahoma 74120

97 96 95 94 93 5 4 3 2 1

Jaffe, David, 1942–

    The New college financial aid system: making it work for you / by David Jaffe.
    p. cm.
    Includes index. ISBN 0–933031–82–3: $14.95
    1. Student aid —United States.   I. Title.
    LB2337.4.J34 1993
    378.3'0973—dc20   93–21692
                                        CIP

Manufactured in the United States of America

ISBN 0-933031-82-3

To Dad,
I know you're proud of me.
This one's for you.

CONTENTS

INTRODUCTION

As college costs continue to rise, more and more families are finding it almost impossible to afford a college education. This problem is not limited to middle income families; even upper income families are finding it difficult to come up with today's costs of tuition. Some families are forced to cash in retirement funds or take a second or third mortgage on their home. Other families have learned the hard way that financial planners rarely take college financial aid into account when planning a financial future. The final result is that most families pay much more for college (sometimes twice the amount) than they would have had to pay with the right advice. Your children will soon be attending college. The college they choose and the career they pursue will have an immeasurable impact on their lives. A decision of this magnitude should be based on academic ability rather than your financial situation. It is for you, middle and upper income families, that this book has been written.

This book contains SIMPLE BOTTOM LINE FACTS THAT WILL SAVE YOU THOUSANDS OF DOLLARS. It explains how the college financial aid system works and the variables that will decide just how much you're going to have to pay. It shows you how to control these variables to greatly increase the amount of financial aid you will receive. To further aid your understanding of the financial aid process, terms appearing in bold type have been included in a comprehensive glossary. From the information provided in this book, you will be able to assemble a plan that will capitalize on your own unique situation. This plan will allow your children to receive a quality education, while protecting the assets and the standard of living you've worked so hard to achieve.

Beginning in the 1950s, university and college officials, including those at the Ivy League colleges, began meeting to exchange information on financial aid and the amounts of the packages being offered to prospective students. The colleges agreed to offer almost identical college financial aid packages to these applicants (based upon their financial need) and therefore not cut their own throats by outbidding each other for desirable students. The colleges claimed that by fixing the cost of education, the prospective students would choose the college of their choice based upon the college itself rather than which college is willing to give them the most financial aid. However, the government did not buy this story and has since stated that financial aid should be available on a competitive basis.

Of 57 institutions investigated, 23 including Brown, Columbia, Cornell, Dartmouth, Penn, Princeton, and Yale have admitted to collaborating with each other and thereby violating the Sherman Antitrust Act. Twenty-two of the 23 colleges accused have settled with the government by agreeing to "never do it again."

Ironically, the information supplied to the colleges in the past to help them "fix" financial aid packages is now *helping* the students get *bigger* and *better* financial aid packages. This is because the colleges are now bidding against each other for desirable students. Now that business has gotten tough for the colleges, there are no holds barred when it comes to signing up a prospective student for four years. Cutting prices by giving rebates in the form of financial aid grants and scholarships is the best way to do this. Just as it is better to sell passage at a discount than to have the plane take off with empty seats, it is better to have full enrollment through the distribution of grants and scholarships than to hold classes and not have them filled. With fewer applicants to college than in years past, it is definitely a buyer's market. There is plenty of money out there. Learn the facts and reap the financial aid awards. That's the bottom line.

1. APPLYING FOR FINANCIAL AID

Who should apply

When it comes to financing a college education, the biggest mistake a family can make is *not* to apply for financial aid. Some parents have been told by well-meaning friends or relatives that if they earn a good living or own real estate, they shouldn't even bother to look for financial assistance. This of course is very bad advice. The **congressional formula** that decides who is eligible for financial aid is a very complicated process that depends on numerous variables. Families that decide on their own that they won't be eligible often are throwing thousands of dollars in grants and loans right out the window. Many families with incomes of over $130,000 per year are receiving **financial aid packages**.

However, what are the psychological ramifications of a middle class family's applying for college financial aid? You must fill out forms. You must answer personal questions. Unfortunately, many people are intimidated by these forms, and some even put college financial aid in the same category as food stamps and welfare. The money is there waiting for them, but they've already been psyched out by the system. The repercussions are incredible. Some of the nation's best minds become the casualty of intimidation. Children who should be applying to Harvard, Princeton, or the finer private schools are applying to less competitive state schools. I wonder how many kids have been sweet-talked into applying to inexpensive colleges because their parents were under the false impression that they would have to hock all of their worldly possessions to send them to the college of their choice. The doctors and scientists who will never be make us all victims of a higher education financing system that intentionally or unintentionally keeps us under-informed and wary of finding out more. Meanwhile, their neighbors who earn as much, if not more than they do, live in the same value home, and have the same amount of assets, are sending their children to the finest and most expensive colleges in the country, and are paying only half as much because they learned the facts about financial aid, planned ahead, and reaped the benefits of their knowledge.

Often, parents will tell me that they have enough money saved to pay for their children's college and would feel guilty if they received financial aid. They say that they don't want to take financial aid funds away from a family that may really need it. Well, nothing could be further from the truth. A family that receives college financial aid is never taking money out of the pockets of a more needy family. Millions of dollars go unused each year because people get bad advice or have improper views about college aid and therefore don't apply.

Who is eligible?

The qualifications for a student receiving college financial aid are the following:

- Have a high school diploma, a **GED**, or have passed an independently administered test approved by the U.S. Department of Education.
- Be enrolled as a **regular student** in an **eligible program**.
- Be enrolled at least **half-time** in an accredited institution.
- Be a **U.S. citizen** or **eligible non-citizen**.

You must also,

- Sign a **Statement of Educational Purpose**.
- Sign a **Certification Statement on Refunds and Default.**
- Sign an **Anti-Drug Abuse Act Certification**.
- Sign a **Statement of Updated Information**.
- Sign a **Statement of Registration Status**.

In order to maintain your aid once you are in college you must make **satisfactory academic progress.**

A person applying for financial aid may also be eligible as an **independent student**. An independent student is one who meets the federal criteria for being financially independent of his or her parents. Financial need is therefore based upon the student's own income and assets, without regard to the finances of his or her parents.

If you claim to be an independent student, your school may ask you to submit proof before you can receive any federal student aid. If you think you have unusual circumstances that would make you independent even though you normally would be considered dependent, talk to the financial aid administrator at your school. The aid administrator can change your status to independent if he or she thinks your circumstances warrant it.

First let's look at the qualifications that will give a student automatic independent status.

1. The student is at least 24 years of age.
2. The student is a **veteran** of the U.S. armed forces.
3. The student is a ward of the court or both parents are dead.
4. The student has **legal dependents** other than a spouse.

Now let's look at the qualifications a student must have to be considered for independent status.

You must not have been claimed as a dependent on your parents' income tax return for the last two years.

A person applying for financial aid may also be eligible as an independent student.

What is financial aid?

College **financial aid** is money to help pay for a college education. This aid comes from the federal government, the state government and the colleges themselves.

The type of aid available falls into three categories:

1. **Grants** (including scholarships)
2. **Loans**
3. **Work-Study** programs

The amount of financial aid that your family is eligible for is determined by a **needs analysis formula**. This formula, which is also known as the congressional formula, takes into account the family's income, assets, and other variables. The result is the **family contribution number**. The family contribution number is the amount of money that the needs analysis formula has determined your family can afford to pay per year for your child's college education. If the total cost of college per year (tuition, room, board, books, fees, laundry, etc.) is higher than your family contribution number, the difference between those two amounts determines your **financial need** or **eligibility**.

For instance. If your family contribution was determined to be $9,000 per year and the cost of the college that you're applying to is $23,000 per year, you would be eligible for $14,000 in financial aid.

Cost of college minus **family contribution** equals **need**.

$$\$23,000-\$9,000=\$14,000$$

Having need and being eligible for financial aid do not guarantee that you will receive financial aid. The amount of financial aid that you receive and the categories in which you receive it are decided by the **financial aid administrator (FAA)** at the college.

Although your family contribution number is the most important factor when putting together a financial aid package, it is not the only factor taken into account. The financial aid administrator may look more closely at your family's financial situation by asking you to fill out additional forms requesting information not previously asked on the federal forms. After all, let's be realistic. The financial aid administrators know that there are loopholes in the system. They know that there are families that receive good financial aid advice and therefore dramatically increase the amount of their financial aid eligibility. Sometimes they try to plug up these loopholes to try to get a more realistic account of what a family can afford. I say "sometimes," because if the student is a very "desirable" student because of scholastic or athletic ability, race, origin, or geographical location, it is in the college's interest to give that student all the financial aid a family is eligible for, and maybe even a little additional money to boot.

As you can see, there is a great "human element" that goes into the making of a financial aid package which is not part of any government program. Most colleges have many financial aid administrators. Some are more generous than others. Upon whose desk your financial aid form lands can be just like a "crap shoot." Sometimes you win a lot. Sometimes you win a little. Sometimes you don't win at all. That's why it's so important to load the dice in your favor and apply to many schools.

Financial aid officers are working *for the college*. Using all the rules of financial aid, their goal is to get you to pay as much as they can get you to pay. You, on the other hand, would like to pay as little as possible. You don't want to have to cash in your IRA. You don't want to have to take out a second or third mortgage on your home. So, it's you against them, but both of you are using the same rules. This book will explain how to use those rules to your advantage.

Financial aid package

This is the total amount of financial aid that a family is being offered for the coming year. This may include state and federal grants including the **Pell Grant** and the **Supplemental Educational Opportunity Grant (SEOG)**. It may also include a **Stafford Loan**, a **Perkins Loan**, or both, and will probably include a **College Work-Study** job. Some colleges may include a **PLUS Loan (Parent's Loans to Undergraduate Students)** in your package, although I don't consider a PLUS Loan to be real financial aid. The interest starts immediately and it has a high maximum interest rate.

A student must be *accepted* at the college before a financial aid package will be sent. This financial aid package is not written in stone and can be reduced if the parent and student tax forms do not match up with the information submitted on the **financial aid form**. The package can also be increased by appealing to the financial aid administrator (FAA) at the college.

College Work-Study

In addition to grants and loans, The **College Work-Study (CWS)** program provides jobs for first time undergraduates and for graduate students that need financial aid. CWS lets you earn money for your educational expenses. The amount of money the student can earn is based on minimum wage, and total earnings cannot exceed the amount of the work-study award.

If you're an undergraduate, you'll be paid by the hour. If you're a graduate student, you may be paid by the hour or you may receive a salary. No CWS student may be paid by commission or fee. Your school must pay you directly at least once a month.

If you work on campus, you'll usually work for your school. If you work off campus, your employer will usually be a private non-profit organization or a local, state, or federal public agency, and the work performed must be in the public interest. Some schools may have agreements with private sector employers for CWS jobs. CWS jobs should be related to your course of study. The school sets your work schedule. When assigning work hours, your financial aid administrator will take into account your class schedule, your health, and your academic progress. And remember, the amount you earn can't exceed your total CWS award.

If I don't want my child to have a job at college, should I turn down the "work-study" program on the financial aid package?

The three components that make up a college financial aid package are grants, loans, and College Work-Study.

Some parents feel that a job at school would be detrimental to their children's studies. These parents can refuse the College Work-Study part of their financial aid package, but then they (the parents) will have to come up with the $50 or $60 per week the work-study would have provided to help pay for weekly out of pocket expenses. You can accept or refuse any part of a financial aid package.

I personally believe that College Work-Study is a big plus for the student. It helps make students feel like they are part of the university. Their social life at school often stems from the work-study job and the 10 or 12 hours a week of work hardly ever interferes with study habits. Give it a try. If it doesn't work out, quit! There are plenty of students who would love to have the job.

However, I suggest that you not turn down any part of a financial aid package. It gives the impression that perhaps you don't need all the financial help that you can get.

When to apply

Apply early. When it comes to receiving free money, be first in line. *Neither* Financial Aid Forms (FAF) *nor* Family Financial Statements (FFS forms) *can be mailed before January 1st.* All federal financial aid forms must be signed and dated after January 1st. Many colleges have deadlines as to when the financial aid form must be sent to its processor. Different colleges have different deadlines. Your best bet is to get it mailed out the first two weeks in January.

Some of these colleges may have their own financial aid forms that are sent directly back to the schools. Make sure that you meet all of these deadlines.

Note: Send all financial aid forms certified mail, return receipt requested. This way you will have proof that all forms were sent on time.

When to plan for college

The full calendar year preceding your child's senior year in high school is the most important year in regard to college financial aid. The only way that the college can get a handle on a family's assets and earnings is to request information from the previous year. The **base income year** in regard to financial aid starts *January 1st* of your *child's junior year* in high school and *extends to December 31st of his or her senior year*. It is this preceding year that your family's financial aid package is based upon.

So . . . don't wait until the last minute. Plan in advance how to shelter your **assets** and those of your children. Plan in advance to "appear" as poor as you legally can. The picture that you present in your base income year will be the foundation for four years of college financial aid. If your child is already beyond December of his or her senior year, don't despair. You can still take advantage of many strategies to increase the amount of your financial aid. Turn to page 27, How to Generate Optimum Financial Aid, for an in-depth look.

Strategies

Things to do before the base income year.

1. Shelter all children's money and trusts by moving it out of their names or into a vehicle that is not counted as an asset by the congressional formula.
2. Shelter parents' excess cash assets into similar vehicles.
3. If you must cash in part of your IRA in order to meet expected college costs, do it before the beginning of your base income year.
4. During the base income year, do not sell anything (stocks, business, etc.) that will show a large **capital gain**. Even though these gains may be a "one time only" item on a tax return, they could knock you out of the box when it comes to financial aid.
5. Don't put your children on the family business payroll. Since up to 50% of your children's income is assessed by the congressional formula, having a child earning a substantial amount of income cannot only reduce the amount of aid that you receive, but could disqualify you completely. To receive the most financial aid, students shouldn't earn more than $1,800 per year.
6. Check into the possibility of having your child apply for an **accelerated program.**

The financial aid cycle

In November or December of your child's senior year in high school, your child will come home from school with a **FAFSA (Free Application for Federal Student Aid)** form plus a **Needs Analysis Form**, which is also called a financial aid form, from one of the **needs analysis services**.

Parents are supposed to fill out this form blindly, not knowing what affect each answer will have on the financial aid package that they will receive. Being in the dark about what makes the college financial aid system work is an advantage to the colleges. For years, parents have filled out financial aid forms and accepted without question the findings of the needs analysis services and the colleges in determining what they will have to pay for their child's college education. After all, these are the higher institutions of learning and we have always held them sacred. Whatever they dictate as to what we will have to pay, we pay. If we were shopping for an expensive car or a $100,000 house, we would certainly shop around and not accept the first price that is thrown at us. But with a college education, it's different. We are conditioned to say, "Thank you for accepting our child, now, how much do we owe you?" However, this doesn't have to be the case.

Most colleges have established their own deadlines for these financial aid forms. The deadlines vary from February 1st to May 1st of your child's senior year of high school. I suggest that financial aid forms be completed and sent to a needs analysis agency as soon after January 1st as possible. I realize that most people haven't received their W-2 forms yet and don't really know what their interest and earnings are for the year. However, speed is more important than having exact accuracy and when it comes to lining up for money, you want to be first. These forms can be filled in based upon an estimate of your assets, income, and interest.

In addition to the FAFSA and the needs analysis forms, many colleges may require you to fill out their own financial aid forms. These forms ask for more information than the government forms do.

After filling out the financial aid form, the form is sent to the government approved processor for evaluation (an addressed envelope is provided). Within six weeks after sending in your financial aid applications, you should receive an acknowledgement from the form processor. This acknowledgment confirms that reports are being sent to all the colleges that you requested they be sent to plus the Pell Grant and state grant agencies in your state. A copy of this report is also sent back to the family. This report is called the **Student Aid Report**. The Student Aid Report contains your estimated family contribution number, your **Pell Grant** eligibility number, a copy of all the questions and answers on the financial aid form, and a confirmation of all of the colleges where this information has been sent. The amount of your financial need will be determined by the amount of the estimated family contribution number deducted from the overall cost of the college.

For example . . . Overall Cost of College minus Family Contribution, equals Financial Need.

Finally, the financial aid administrators at the college will put all of this information into their brains and decide just how much of your need eligibility can be met with financial aid, and the types (loans, grants, Work-Study) and amounts of this financial aid.

Remember, having financial need does *not* guarantee receiving financial aid.

Meet those deadlines

Not meeting a deadline or not having proof of meeting a deadline can be a disaster. Most of the colleges that you are applying to will have different deadlines so you must pay attention. Always send "deadline mail" certified, return receipt requested. This is the only way that you can prove that you met the deadline if your papers get lost.

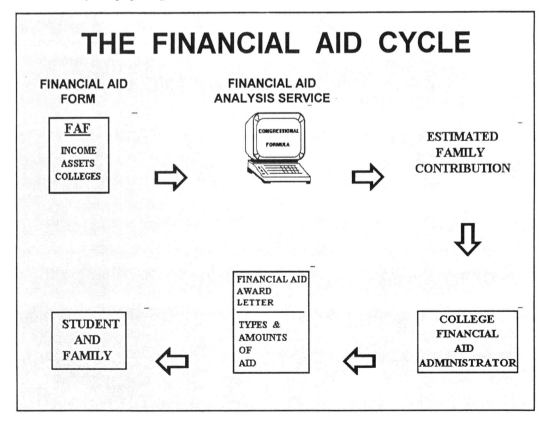

It is very likely that you may find yourself in a situation where the acceptance deadline at a college is coming up but you're still waiting to hear from another college that you would rather attend. When this is the situation, call the school and see if you can get an extension on the deadline date. Many colleges will give you a two week extension, but that might not be enough. If this is the case, send in your acceptance and deposit check. If you end up changing your mind after receiving information from another college, there is a chance that you might get your check back. If you don't get it back, write it off as part of the expense of applying for college.

A note to transfer students

All transfer students intending to apply for financial aid will have to have a financial aid transcript sent from the college that they are transferring from (including all colleges previously attended) to all of the colleges that they are planning to transfer to. Even if you received no financial aid at a previous school, a transcript still must be sent.

Deadlines may be different for transfer students than they are for freshmen or regular undergraduate students. Check with the financial aid offices at the colleges to which you are applying for transfer. The financial aid transcripts that you will need are also available through these offices. You must send these financial aid transcript forms to the colleges that you have attended, and follow up to make sure these forms are filled out and sent back to the financial aid offices at the schools to which you are applying. Even if you received no financial aid from a previous college, the form still must be sent before a college can give a transfer student a financial aid package. They will want to see just how much aid you were receiving at a previous college. Since certain aid programs have an aggregate limit (Stafford and Perkins Loans) the college must know how much you have already received in order to know what is still available to you.

Transfer tips for financial aid

Never transfer in the middle of the year. Most financial aid funds have been committed for the year and the college will tell you there is no money available.

When transferring, always apply to more than one school. This lets a school know that they are competing for you and must at least match the other school's financial aid offer if they want you to fill a seat at their institution.

Before going any further, review this checklist to ensure the most expeditious way of paving the financial road to the college of your choice.

Financial aid checklist

1. Select colleges.
2. Contact colleges for application and financial aid deadline dates.
3. Carefully complete all parts of the financial aid form. Don't leave any blanks. If the answer doesn't apply, put in a 0 so the needs analysis service knows that you did not leave it blank by mistake. This can save you the time of having to answer an inquiry letter.
4. Keep copies of everything that is sent in regard to admissions and financial aid.
5. Send all forms certified mail, return receipt requested.
6. Receive Student Aid Report. Check report for accuracy and send a copy to the financial aid office at all of the colleges that you have applied to. The original copy of the Student Aid Report will be sent to the college that you eventually choose.
7. If the college or the needs analysis service requires additional information, send it promptly.
8. Receive Financial Aid Award Letter. Read it carefully and if you have any questions, *call the college*.
9. Accept all or part of your financial aid award. Sign and return your award to the college.
10. Complete enrollment and registration procedures at the college.

2. EARLY DECISIONS AND SCHOLARSHIPS

Early decision admissions

This is a plan that is offered to applicants that are sure of the school that they want to attend and feel that they have an excellent chance of being accepted. Students are notified of the college's decision by December 15th of their senior year of high school. This is much earlier than the usual acceptance dates of March 1st through May 1st. Accepting an **early decision** will not only require the students to commit themselves to attend that college, but also will require them to withdraw all other college applications.

When it comes to college financial aid, early decision is usually the wrong way to go. Since colleges are competing fiercely for fewer and fewer students, it makes sense to apply to many colleges (some high schools require that the students send out seven or eight college applications). The colleges are aware of all the other schools that you are applying to, and they even know the order of preference that they are listed (this information is supplied to them by the needs analysis agency). This puts the colleges in a position of *bidding* for you to fill the seat at their institution. For instance . . . if College X is listed as your third choice on your financial aid form and College X feels that you will be accepted at your first two choices, College X knows that it must offer you an *incentive* for you to choose it. This *incentive* may come in the form of a financial grant that the school feels will be much higher than your first two choices in order to "steal you away." As you can see, applying for early decision puts the college in a position of having no other colleges to compete with. It can offer you less aid and still be assured that you will accept its offer. This is great for the college but not so great for the applicant. Although early decision does simplify the whole admissions process and does eliminate a lot of applications and paper work, *it is not worth it!* Getting a good financial aid package in your freshman year is paramount, because even though you have to reapply for financial aid each year, you sort of "make your bed" in the first year for the three years that will follow.

Scholarships

Scholarship. It's a great word. It brings visions of the poor and underprivileged having their lives turned around by winning or being presented with a "scholarship."

Unfortunately, the only people who really benefit financially from scholarships are the rich who can afford to go to college and pay full tuition in the first place, and the colleges themselves. The poor and underprivileged, whom we all visualize as gaining the most from scholarship programs, are the people it helps the least.

The American public has been led to believe that scholarships can be the answer for families too poor to afford a good college education. Almost all the clubs, corporations, and organizations that give out scholarships are under the impression that they are helping a worthy student or his family pay for a college education. This is exactly what the colleges want them to think. The truth of the matter is that if you are poor or middle class, the scholarship that you receive will not put any money in your pocket or even reduce the amount of your college tuition bill...

In reality, the family of the student that receives a "scholarship" has to pay the same price that it would have had to pay if the student didn't receive the scholarship in the first place. Instead of the scholarship subsidizing the student for whom the money was originally intended, the scholarship subsidizes the colleges.

Let me show you a classic example of how all this works.

Larry had his heart set on going to his state university which cost $9,500 per year. After filling out all the proper financial aid forms, the university advised Larry's family that according to their needs analysis, Larry's family could afford to contribute $4,000 towards that cost. The university would give them a financial aid package of $4,000 in university grants and $1,500 in federal loans.

The financial aid package looked fine to Larry's family, however, the $4,000 that Larry's family would have to contribute would be quite a strain on the family finances. What could they do? Larry's mom got an idea. The corporation where she worked as a bookkeeper awarded two $2,500 college scholarships each year to the children of employees who showed merit and need. Larry's mom found out that the scholarships had not been awarded yet and came home the next day with a load of papers for Larry and his parents to fill out.

They sat up that night filling out the forms, and the next day his mother delivered them at work. Three day's later Larry was interviewed by the Board of Directors at the corporation. Each day he waited for the mail to arrive and on the fifth day, he received the letter that informed him that he had indeed won the $2,500 scholarship. The family was ecstatic. They went out to dinner that night to celebrate, and the next day Larry sent his $2,500 scholarship award letter on to the financial aid administrator at the university. Two weeks later, Larry received a letter from the financial aid office at the university. It said "Thank you very much for bringing this scholarship with you to State University. This scholarship will be lowering your need by $2,500. Enclosed, please find your *revised* fianancial award."

After all that hassle, Larry's family contribution had not changed. It was going to cost him the same $4,000 to attend the university as it would have before he received the $2,500 scholarship. The only one to gain from the scholarship was the university itself.

Now, I could have told you this story in just a few sentences, but I wanted to drive home the point that people go to *a lot of trouble* to get these scholarships thinking that this is the answer to their financial woes. Obviously it is not. The way to get the most financial aid is to present your family's financial situation in the most favorable way possible. The lower your family's income and assets, the more financial help you're going to get.

The system is not going to change. If clubs, organizations, and corporations really want to help their employees or those who are gifted and in need, they should give the scholarship money to the students after the students graduate. This way the money can be used for graduate school or living expenses without being detrimental to their undergraduate financial aid package. In this way scholarship winners can really reap the rewards.

Scholarship search services

Often **scholarship search services** prove to be a waste of time, energy, and money. All of these services work from the same computer program to match you up with available scholarship funds based on everything from being left-handed to having an interest in frogs and turtles. The problem is that when you take the time and energy to write these people, in many cases, you don't even get an answer. Most of the people I know of who have used these services have received nothing in the way of scholarship money. Be especially wary of companies that "guarantee" scholarships and grants. If you read the fine print you will realize that it's virtually impossible to prove that you never received any scholarships. If after reading this, you are still tempted to try one of these scholarship services, call the Better Business Bureau in your area.

The ironic thing is that even if you do receive a scholarship award, the financial aid administrator at the college will only deduct it from your forthcoming financial aid package. So...searching for scholarships is not the answer to financing your college education. The way to finance it is to present your family's financial situation in the most favorable way possible. The lower your income and assets, the more financial aid you're going to get.

Remember, if you do receive a scholarship it is something to be proud of, and the college will be most appreciative. In fact, the college may be so appreciative that instead of deducting the scholarship from intended grant money, they may deduct it from loan money instead. If this is the case, then your scholarship will be a financial gain. But don't count on it.

Need blind admissions

When a college has a **need blind admissions** policy, it means that the admissions decision will be based entirely upon the student's academic ability, character, and ability to succeed at college. In past years it was automatically assumed that the college would come up with enough financial aid to fill the potential student's need. However, need blind admissions are slowly becoming a thing of the past. Many colleges are now reviewing a student's financial aid form and the family's ability to pay before accepting the applicant. Many of these colleges lack the funds to give every eligible student a financial aid package that will satisfy his or her need. Some colleges start off each year being need blind until all available funds run out. At that point, a student's ability to pay will come into play. That is why it is so important to apply early to the college and to apply as early as possible for financial aid. It's first come, first served.

Other colleges may take "ability to pay" into consideration for all applicants right from the beginning. In this situation, the wealthy student who requires no aid will definitely have an advantage when it comes to being accepted. Because of this fact, many families anxious to have a child accepted at a certain college may not apply for financial aid because they think it will be detrimental to the child's acceptance. This deprives many families of financial aid that they really would have qualified for and would have received. Don't let these revelations scare you into not applying for aid. Chances are your inability to pay won't influence your child's acceptance. Go for the money.

3. HOW TO GENERATE OPTIMUM FINANCIAL AID

By planning in advance and using the methods shown in the following chapter, families can save thousands of dollars in college costs. What it requires is that the family demonstrate a need in terms the financial aid officers will recognize. To do this, you must first take into consideration certain variables which are the backbone of the financial aid package. They are:

1. The age of the student's parents.
2. The size of the student's household.
3. Incomes of parents and student.
4. Value of home and real estate.
5. Savings and other investments.
6. Number of persons in the student's family attending college.
7. Parents' marital status.
8. Opening or owning your own farm or business.
9. Choice of school.

The first two variables, "the age of the student's parents" and "the size of the student's household," obviously cannot be controlled. However, variables 3 through 9, in many instances can be controlled.

Manipulating the variables

Variable 3: Incomes of parents and student

For families that don't own their own business, income is pretty cut and dry. I suggest postponing any December or Christmas bonus income (if possible) until January of the following year. Aside from this, there is nothing else that you can really do. However, you will be happy to know that before the parents' earnings are assessed, a portion of their income will be automatically sheltered by an **income protection allowance**. The amount of parents' income that is sheltered is dependent on the size of the family household and how many family members are attending college at least half-time.

The table below shows the amount sheltered by the income protection allowance for *each* college student in the family.

INCOME PROTECTION ALLOWANCE						
Family Size	Number in College					
(including student)	1	2	3	4	5	For each additional subtract
2	10,520	8,720				1,790
3	13,100	11,310	9,510			
4	16,180	14,380	12,590	10,790		
5	19,090	17,290	15,500	13,700	11,910	
6	22,330	20,530	18,740	16,940	15,150	
For each addl. add	2,510	2,510	2,510	2,510	2,510	

Source: House of Representatives conference report, Higher Education Amendments of 1992.

The student's *entire* income, however, is subject to a congressional formula. According to the government, every student must work and contribute towards his or her college education. The formula dictates that every student should earn up to $1,800 at a summer job, $900 of which should be put aside for college tuition. This $900 will be added to the parents' family contribution. Even if a student doesn't work during summer vacation, $900 will automatically be added. The $900 amount is for entering freshmen only. For sophomores, juniors, and seniors, the automatic amount is $1,100. Some colleges put in up to $1,350 for the student's previous summer earnings whether the student earns money or not. It may seem, therefore, that a student should earn as much as possible since only $900-$1,350 will be counted against his or her aid award. However, if a student earns more than $1,800 per year, 50% of everything over that amount will also be added to the family contribution. In other words, if your child has a great summer job or is put on the family business payroll and earns $5,000, the congressional formula will add a total of $2,500 to your family contribution. Since this is the case, a low paying job may be a better choice for your college bound student.

Variable 4: Value of home and real estate

Starting in the 1993-1994 school year, the value of your family's home will no longer be taken into consideration by the congressional formula. This means that the equity in your home (the value of your home minus what is owed on it) will no longer be a factor in calculating a family's need for college financial aid. Even though your **home equity** has been eliminated from the federal formula, most colleges will still want to know about your home value and will take its equity into consideration when figuring out the amount of a financial aid package.

The biggest mistake that families make is to over-estimate the value of their homes, especially in the current real estate market. By using the government's own formula of **minimum derived value**, you can usually lower the estimated worth of real estate substantially while staying within the government's own guidelines. To find the minimum derived value of your home or property, use the multiplier supplied by the U.S. Department of Commerce, Bureau of Economic Analysis (see p. 30).

Remember, many families have thought that their homes were worth for-tunes until they tried to sell them. Then they learned the true value. Don't assume your house is worth the same as the house down the block that was just sold. The person who bought your neighbor's house may have been a fool. The government's own definition of **home value** is not the tax value or the appraised value, but the price you would get if you were to sell your home tomorrow. In the present real estate market, if no one has made you an offer on your house, it's value should be determined using the government's own formula.

Although the federal **Housing Index multiplier** gives a very conservative value of your home, there are places in the country and extenuating circum-stances under which a home bought 15 years ago is worth the same or less than when purchased. If this is the case, state the lower value of your home but be prepared to explain to the FAA why your home has not appreciated in value. Example...living in a flood area or near a highway.

The Housing Index and Commercial Property Index multiplier chart on page 30 will give you the minimum acceptable value for your home or commercial property. Here's how to use it:

Take the year of purchase of your home or commercial property (year of valuation) and multiply the purchase price by the number directly to the right. Example . . . If you purchased a home in 1976, you will multiply the purchase price by 2.21. If you purchased commercial property in 1976, then you would multiply the purchase price by 2.15.

MULTIPLIERS

Year of Valuation	Housing Index Multiplier	Commercial Property Index Multiplier
1958	4.51	4.76
1959	4.51	4.83
1960	4.48	4.83
1961	4.48	4.83
1962	4.46	4.80
1963	4.50	4.71
1964	4.48	4.63
1965	4.42	4.50
1966	4.27	4.32
1967	4.17	4.32
1968	3.97	4.02
1969	3.62	3.66
1970	3.52	3.45
1971	3.32	3.17
1972	3.13	2.94
1973	2.86	2.73
1974	2.58	2.45
1975	2.38	2.24
1976	2.21	2.15
1977	1.96	2.00
1978	1.73	1.82
1979	1.54	1.63
1980	1.39	1.48
1981	1.29	1.36
1982	1.26	1.29
1983	1.23	1.24
1984	1.19	1.18
1985	1.16	1.15
1986	1.13	1.11
1987	1.07	1.07
1988	1.04	1.03
1989*	1.00	1.00

Homes and property purchased after 1989 should be valued at the purchase price.

To make sure that you don't undervalue your property, it is a good idea to add an extra 10% to the value dictated by the multiplier.

Variable 5: Savings and other investments

When computing the family contribution, the congressional formula will assess approximately 12% of the parents' assets and 35% of the student's assets for the previous base year. Before parents' assets are assessed at the 12% rate, they are allowed an asset protection allowance of many thousands of dollars. Students receive no such allowance and therefore are assessed 35% of every dollar they have and everything they own. That's why *the movement of a student's money can be one of the most important factors in lowering the cost of college*. If the student's money is transferred to the parents' name, then the college will compute only 12% of whatever amount is above the asset protection allowance when determining the family contribution rather than 35% of the entire asset.

Another way to make the student's money "disappear" from the congressional formula is to invest it in a **tax deferred annuity** or in a **single premium life insurance policy**. In any case, the student's money must be moved or you can kiss it all goodbye. Movement of these funds should be made at least two years before the student graduates from high school. The reason for this is that some colleges may ask for tax forms dating back two years to see if there is an interest trail from the student's money that may have been moved for purposes of college financial aid. Although most colleges don't ask for back copies of tax forms, some colleges do.

Parents with more than $50,000 in liquid assets should also consider the movement of their assets into a tax deferred annuity or single premium life insurance policy because the financial aid officer at the college may decide that you look too rich and hold back some of the aid that you are eligible to receive. Remember, the financial aid officer at the college has the last word as to what your financial aid package will be.

Manipulating these variables is a safe, legal way to ensure that your application for financial aid is seen in the best possible light. By taking these few simple steps into account, you will create optimum financial need to enable your children to attend their college of choice.

The following tables will show you how much of your family's assets are sheltered before the 12% assessment begins. As you can see, it is based on the age of the older parent. Example . . . If the older parent is 45 years old, then the first $36,600 of assets is sheltered. For a single parent also 45 years of age, the first $26,300 is sheltered.

EDUCATION SAVINGS AND ASSET PROTECTION ALLOWANCES
FOR FAMILIES AND STUDENTS

	Allowance for:	
Age of oldest parent	**_two parent family_**	**_one parent family_**
25 or under	$ 0	$ 0
26	2,200	2,200
27	4,300	3,200
28	6,500	4,700
29	8,600	6,300
30	10,800	7,900
31	13,000	9,500
32	15,100	11,100
33	17,300	12,600
34	19,400	14,200
35	21,600	15,800
36	23,800	17,400
37	25,900	19,000
38	28,100	20,500
39	30,200	22,100
40	32,400	23,700
41	33,300	24,100
42	34,100	24,700
43	35,000	25,200
44	35,700	25,800
45	36,600	26,300
46	37,600	26,900
47	38,800	27,600
48	39,800	28,200
49	40,800	28,800
50	41,800	29,500
51	43,200	30,200
52	44,300	31,100
53	45,700	31,800
54	47,100	32,600
55	48,300	33,400
56	49,800	34,400
57	51,300	35,200
58	52,900	36,200
59	54,800	37,200
60	56,500	38,100
61	58,500	39,200
62	60,300	40,300
63	62,400	41,500
64	64,600	42,800
65 or over	66,800	44,000

Variable 6: How many will attend college?

One of the most important questions in determining your family contribution is "How many in college?" When answering, most families assume that the question relates only to the children. This is a false assumption. Parents who plan to attend college and list themselves as also going to school quite often can reduce the cost of their children's college by as much as 50%. According to the congressional formula, a parent attending college half-time (six credits for one semester), for example, will have the same positive affect on your family contribution as having another child attending college. The courses that the parents take do not have to go towards a degree, as long as they are college accredited. You can take courses in whatever interests you, and the few hundred dollars that you invest in furthering your own education can save you thousands of dollars on the cost of your children's education. This factor alone has often made the difference between a family paying $90,000 or $45,000 for the same four years of college. To insure your credibility, it is best for the parent to start attending classes six months before the children are scheduled to begin college. By the way, you don't have to pass these courses to receive the financial credit on your children's college costs. You just have to *attend*.

If you have an older child who has graduated from college, dropped out of college, or never attended, have him or her plan to take six credits of undergraduate or postgraduate courses in one semester. This will also have the same positive affect on your younger child's college costs because every additional college student in the family lowers your family contribution. I cannot emphasize enough how important this variable is in determining your family contribution number.

Again I want to emphasize that we are not pulling the wool over anybody's eyes. The financial aid officers at the colleges are well aware of the affect that a parent in college has on a family contribution number. However, because it does increase the amount of financial aid eligibility, it allows the college's financial aid officers the latitude to offer you a bigger financial aid package if they wish.

Having discussed the variables which will generate optimum financial aid, let's take a look at a case study we'll call "the Goodmans."

CASE STUDY #1

Michael and Michelle Goodman are a typical middle class couple. They live in the suburbs, have two children, Adam and Stacy, and both children are attending high school. Adam is a junior and Stacy is a freshman. Both parents work, and their combined income totals about $65,000 per year. They purchased their home in 1976 for $80,000 and estimate its worth to be about $300,000. They still owe $40,000 on the first mortgage and have a second mortgage of $80,000. The total debt on the house is $120,000. They have about $30,000 in savings and each child has $10,000 in college funds in their own names.

Adam would like to attend a private college where the cost is $22,000 per year. However, the Goodmans don't really believe they can afford this.

They do know that they can afford a state college where the total cost per year is $9,500, but they are also aware that Adam will be heart-broken if he cannot attend the private college which is the school of his choice.

Even though the Goodmans had been told by all their friends that they would never be able to qualify for college financial aid, they still made an appointment with a college financial aid counselor who was recommended by a friend at work. The financial aid counselor took all the information needed and ran it through the government's financial aid formula.

At first glance, it certainly looks as though the Goodmans' friends are right and they won't qualify for financial aid. According to the congressional formula, the Goodmans can afford to pay $25,000 a year for Adam's college education and since the cost of the school is only $22,000 per year, there is certainly no *need* for financial aid.

So, what can the Goodmans do? With the help of the financial aid counselor, they can use the variables in order to demonstrate *need*. The result will be an outstanding financial aid package.

First, the counselor wants to get the lowest value possible on the Goodmans' home so he takes the year that the Goodmans bought their home (1976) and the price that they paid for it ($80,000) and runs the figures through the government's own formula of minimum derived value. According to the government's formula, the value of the Goodmans' home is $195,000. That is $105,000 less than the Goodmans would have declared.

Note: Although a family's home equity is not considered to be an asset in the congressional formula, most colleges take home equity into consideration when constructing a financial aid package.

Second, the counselor now suggests that the Goodmans take Adam's $10,000 out of his name and transfer it to their name. This will further reduce the Goodmans' family contribution because the $10,000 will now be assessed at the parental rate of 12% instead of the student rate of 35%.

Third, the counselor convinces Mrs. Goodman that if she takes six credits of classes at the local college, it will have a very positive affect on Adam's financial aid. So, instead of listing Adam as the only family member planning to go to college next year, they also list his mother. This gives them two family members attending college, which means that their income protection allowance will be increased considerably.

Now, when the financial aid counselor runs the new figures through the government's financial aid formula, the Goodmans' expected family contribution is reduced to $10,500.

Since the cost of education at the private college is $22,000 and the Goodman's family contribution is now $10,500, the Goodmans are now eligible for $11,500 in college financial aid. All the financial aid counselor did to determine this amount was use the equation:

Cost of College	minus	Family Contribution	equals	Eligibility of Need
22,000		10,500		11,500

The result is that the Goodmans receive over $10,500 per year in college financial aid of which $8,000 per year is in grants (free money that doesn't have to be paid back). The other $2,500 is a guaranteed student loan that doesn't have to be paid back until after Adam graduates from college. And most importantly, Adam can attend the college of his choice.

Let's look at other various scenarios which will come under scrutiny when you apply for college aid.

Variable 7: Marital status

In my years of consulting, one of the things that I find to be most interesting is the great advantage that separated and divorced families seem to have when it comes to financial aid awards. Some parents give away this advantage by voluntarily supplying too much information to the colleges and the College Scholarship Service. According to the congressional formula, the family contribution is based on the **custodial parent** or the parent that the child lives with most of the year. It is *this* parent's income and assets *alone*, plus the income and assets of the student that determine the family contribution number. It is a fact of life in America that some parents just step out of the picture and let their ex-spouses fend for themselves. It is *so* common that most colleges will just accept this fact. Here's an example.

CASE STUDY #2

Steven and Claudia Smith and their three children lived in New York City. They owned a duplex apartment in which Steven lived upstairs and Claudia lived downstairs. The Smiths were separated but it seemed economically wise and much less of a hassle to keep their assets together and to continue to file a joint tax return.

Their daughter Debra was 15 years old and was just finishing up her sophomore year in high school. Their twins, Erick and Josh, were 13 and would be entering high school the following year.

Steven worked for the Board of Education and earned about $60,000 per year. Claudia worked for the Department of Social Services and earned about $30,000 per year. Their interest and dividends from savings and stocks earned them another $10,000 per year. Their total income was about $100,000 per year.

The family's assets included their home, which was worth about $200,000. However, they still owed about $100,000 on the mortgage, so the equity in the house was about $100,000. Their savings and investments totalled another $150,000, and they owned a country house worth about $60,000. The children, Debra, Erick, and Josh, each had a trust fund of $20,000 each from their grandparents.

For purposes of college financial aid, this is what the family's income and assets looked like.

Steven and Claudia's income	$90,000
Interest income	$10,000
Home equity	$100,000
Other real estate	$60,000
Money in children's names	$60,000

Looking at these figures it seems that Steven and Claudia were somewhat financially secure. They earned $100,000 per year, had over $250,000 in assets and had an extra $60,000 in trusts to help pay for the children's college. However, being financially secure was about as far from reality as they could have been.

The reality was that even though Steven and Claudia earned over $100,000 per year, after taxes, mortgage, insurance, and private high school costs, there was nothing left over, yet their income and financial status made them ineligible for any college financial aid.

Steven and Claudia knew that the children would be starting college in three years and if they went to the colleges of their choice, the costs would be about $21,000 *each* per year. The total cost for the three children would be about $252,000. Everything the Smiths had worked and saved for was about to be wiped out in order to educate their children. They would have to take a second mortgage on their home and cash in most of their liquid assets. College costs were going to turn financial security into financial disaster.

Steven and Claudia took their problem to a well qualified financial planner. On the advice of this financial planner, Steven and Claudia decided to "really" split. That's right! They became legally separated. They split all their property. They each owned half of the city house and the country house and their stocks were split into two separate accounts. The three $20,000 trusts in the children's names were invested in **single premium insurance deposits (SPIDs)** to be sheltered for the next seven years.

Now their income and assets looked like this.

Claudia's Income and Assets	*Steven's Income and Assets*
Income 30,000	Income 60,000
Interest 5,000	Interest 5,000
Home equity 50,000	Home equity 50,000
Investments 62,500	Investments 61,500
Real estate 30,000	Real estate 30,000
Children's assets 0	Children's assets 0

Claudia received college financial aid for Debra based upon her income and assets only. According to the congressional formula, the children's trusts were no longer considered an asset since they were transferred into single premium insurance deposits.

Claudia eventually received about $144,000 in college grants (free money) and $48,000 in interest free loans (Loans are "interest free" as long as the children are in school. Interest begins six months after they leave or graduate). Claudia had to pay about $5,000 per year, per child, for the best college education money could buy. The children's trusts which were not used for school ($20,000 each) totalled $60,000 and were cashed in after seven years at a worth of over $80,000. This money was used to pay off the student loans.

Divorced parents

According to the congressional formula, the income and assets of the non-custodial parent are *not* part of the formula that determines the amount of your financial aid eligibility. In past years only a small minority of colleges, including all of the Ivy League schools, asked for information on the non-custodial parent. However, more and more schools have been asking for this information because many colleges realize that families use this loophole to greatly lower college costs. Colleges asking for information that is not part of the federal formula may be hoping that you will supply them with enough information (or rope) to hang yourself. They will either ask for this additional information on their own financial aid application or they will send the custodial parent a form called the **Divorced/Separated Parent's Statement**. They will ask the custodial parent to forward this form on to the non-custodial parent.

In my opinion, unless the non-custodial parent is unemployed and flat broke, this form can only hurt you. Many people get away with not filling out this form by claiming that there is no contact with their previous spouse or so little co-operation that the ex-spouse will not acknowledge even receiving the form. Since this is honestly the case in many instances, it is impossible for the college to know who is telling the truth and who is not. Believe it or not, the best case scenario in this situation is to be deserted by your ex-spouse and not receive either child support or alimony.

With many schools, it becomes a judgment call as to whether or not you are telling the truth about your ex-spouse. In the case of no cooperation from an ex-spouse, it is best to write a letter and explain your situation. If you have any documents or lawyer's letters to help support your case, send them along. Wait a week and then follow up with a phone call. It is the financial aid officer who decides whether or not to include your ex-spouse when deciding the amount of your financial aid package.

According to the federal formula, there is absolutely no difference at all between being separated, legally separated, or divorced. However, the difference of being divorced or separated and the amount of time that has elapsed since your divorce or separation can make a difference to the FAA who is deciding the amount of your financial aid package. Let's face it. A divorce of 15 years is a lot more credible than a separation of just one year. The FAA may feel that a separation of just one year may have been created strictly for the benefits of college financial aid. In many cases they would be 100% right.

Divorced/Separated Parent's Statement

School Year 1993-94

CONFIDENTIAL

This form is to be filed by the noncustodial parent.

Return it directly to the college providing the statement.

College Scholarship Service
THE COLLEGE BOARD

Instructions for Completing the Parent's Statement

Because you are asked to give financial information on this form, you should get these records together:
- 1992 U.S. income tax return (IRS Form 1040, 1040A, or 1040EZ)
- W-2 forms and other records of money earned in 1992
- Current mortgage information
- Records of medical and other expenses paid in 1992
- Business and farm records
- Records of social security, veterans, or other benefits

The U.S. income tax return will be especially helpful.

If you have not completed a 1992 U.S. income tax return, you will have to estimate what will be reported on it.

If you will not file an income tax return, you will need to know how much nontaxable income (such as social security or welfare benefits) your family received in 1992.

For questions asking about 1993, you should give the best possible estimate of income.

Because some of the questions are self-explanatory, the instructions below are only for questions that may need some explanation.

Section II — Parent's (and Current Spouse's) Information

6. Write in the number of people in your (and current spouse's) household during 1993-94. Include yourself, your current spouse (if any), and dependent children. Include other people only if they now live with you and get more than half their support from you.

7. Write in the number of people from question 6 who will attend college at least half-time during 1993-94. Half-time means a student is taking at least six credit hours a term.

Section III — Parent's (and Current Spouse's) Annual Income and Expenses

For some of the questions in Section III, it may be helpful to refer to the U.S. income tax return (IRS Form 1040, 1040A, or 1040EZ).

If you did not (or will not) file a U.S. income tax return, write in "0" for questions that do not apply to you.

9. a-f. Write in the total amounts. When any amount is from more than one source, list the kinds and amounts of income in Section V, "Remarks."

Here are references for the 1991 IRS Form 1040, 1040A, and 1040EZ as they relate to questions 9a-f.

	The IRS line references below are for 1991. For 1992 use the corresponding lines from IRS Form 1040, 1040A, or 1040EZ.		
	1991 line references		
Question	Form 1040	Form 1040A	Form 1040EZ
9a	7	7	1
9b	8a	8a	2
9c	9	9	—
9d	12, 19	—	—
9e	10, 11, 13-15, 16b, 17b, 18, 20, 21b, 22	10b, 11b, 12, 13b	—
9f	30	15c	—

10. Write in the amounts of nontaxable income from:

a. Untaxed portion of social security benefits (Include only amounts that you get for yourself, your current spouse, and dependent children under age 18.)

b. All other income, such as:
- Child support received
- Welfare benefits
- Veterans benefits
- Interest on tax-free bonds
- Untaxed portions of pensions
- Housing and living allowances for military, clergy, and others (Include cash payments and cash value of benefits.)
- Any other income that is not included in any other question

11. Write in the amount of U.S. income tax paid (or to be paid). Refer to 1992 IRS Form 1040, 1040A, or 1040EZ. Do not copy the amount of "federal income tax withheld" from a W-2 Form. Do not include taxes paid on earnings from student financial aid programs.

12.– 14. Write in the total amounts. If you itemized deductions on the 1992 U.S. income tax return, you may refer to the following lines of IRS Form 1040, Schedule A:

	The IRS line references below are for 1991. For 1992 use the corresponding lines from IRS Schedule A.
	1991 line references
Question	Form 1040, Schedule A
12	26
13	8*
14	1
	*Add Sales Tax

12. Write in the amount of itemized deductions from the U.S. income tax return. If you did not (or will not) itemize deductions or you did not (or will not) file a return, write in "0."

13. Write in the amount paid (or to be paid) for state and local taxes. Include state and local income, real estate, sales, personal property, and other taxes.

14. Write in the amount of medical and dental expenses paid in 1992. Include the cost of medicine, drugs, and other medical and dental expenses (doctors, dentists, nurses, hospital, etc.) that are not paid by insurance. Also include the cost of insurance premiums for medical and dental care. Don't include amounts covered by insurance, your company medical reimbursement account (flexible spending account), or self-employed health deductions.

15. Write in the total amount of other unusual expenses, such as payments for child support, outstanding medical and dental expenses, expenses associated with a disability, funerals, legal fees, and water, street, and sewer assessments. List the kinds and amounts of expenses in Section V, "Remarks."

Section IV — Parent's (and Current Spouse's) Assets and Debts

17.– 21. Write in the information requested regarding each form of asset. In questions 17, 18, and 21, "present market value" means the amount that the asset could currently be sold for. Do not use valuations such as assessed value, insured value, or tax value.

Do not report any asset more than once. If you jointly own assets with your former spouse, include only your (and your current spouse's) portion of the assets and debts.

22. Write in the amount of any debt outstanding. Do not include any expenses or debts that are already included in questions 15-21. Include such **past** debts as medical and dental expenses; remaining business indebtedness, if business dissolved; funeral expenses; legal fees; unreimbursed job-related moving expenses; natural disasters not covered by insurance; liens; living expenses, if business failure, prolonged illness, or unemployment has depleted assets and forced indebtedness; and your educational indebtedness. Do not include any other kind of debt outstanding.

Section V — Remarks

In this section give any explanations or detailed listings of financial entries that were asked for earlier in the form. You may also give information regarding any circumstances that you believe should be considered in evaluating the student applicant's need for financial aid. Be specific; give complete details, including dollar amounts and explanations.

Section VI — Certification and Authorization

You must sign this form. In signing this form, you certify that all the information on the form is correct and complete and that you are willing to provide documents (such as a U.S. income tax return) to prove that the information is correct and complete.

Please double-check this Parent's Statement to make sure that it is complete and accurate. Be sure that it has the required signature.

DIVORCED/SEPARATED PARENT'S STATEMENT

School Year 1993-94

Return this form directly to the college that provided it.

Section I — Student Applicant Information

1. a. Student's name — Last _____ First _____ M.I. ___   **b.** Student's social security number ___ – ___ – ___

Section II — Parent's (and Current Spouse's) Information

2. Student's parent

a. Name_____ b. Age_____

c. Street address_____

City, State, Zip code_____

d. Occupation_____

e. Title_____

f. Employer_____

g. Number of years with employer_____

h. Are you covered by this employer's pension plan? yes ☐ no ☐

i. State of legal residence_____

j. Social security number ___ – ___ – ___

3. Parent's current spouse (if any)

a. Name_____ b. Age_____

c. Street address_____

City, State, Zip code_____

d. Occupation_____

e. Title_____

f. Employer_____

g. Number of years with employer_____

h. Are you covered by this employer's pension plan? yes ☐ no ☐

i. State of legal residence_____

j. Social security number ___ – ___ – ___

4. Parent's support of former household

a. Name of person who claimed student as a dependent on most recent U.S. income tax return

_____

	1992	1993
b. Annual child support paid for all children	$_____.00	$_____.00
c. Annual child support paid for the student applicant	$_____.00	$_____.00
d. When will (did) student applicant's support end? _____		
e. Alimony paid	$_____.00	$_____.00
f. What do you expect to contribute to the student applicant's education in addition to child support?	$_____.00	$_____.00

Parent's current household

5. Total number of exemptions claimed or expected to be claimed on parent's U.S. income tax return for

... 1992 _____   ... 1993 _____

6. The total size of the parent's household during 1993-94 will be .... ☐ (Include the parent, the parent's current spouse (if any) and parent's other dependent children. Include other dependents if they meet the definition in the instructions.)

7. Of the number in **6**, how many will be in college during 1993-94? (Include only persons who will be enrolled at least half-time.) ☐

8. Give information for all individuals included in parent's household in **6**. Include the parent and the parent's current spouse (if any). For persons not in school, complete name and age only.

Name	Age	Educational information, 1992-93					Educational information, 1993-94			
		Name of school or college, 1992-93	Year in school or college	Tuition and fees	Room and board	Scholarships and gift aid	Parent's contribution	Name of school or college, 1993-94	full-time	half-time or more	less than half-time

If more space is needed, continue in Section V, "Remarks."

Section III — Parent's (and Current Spouse's) Annual Income and Expenses

9. Total **taxable income** (See instructions.) The following income figures are:

☐ from a completed 1992 IRS Form 1040A or 1040EZ   ☐ from a completed 1992 IRS Form 1040   ☐ estimated, a 1992 tax return will be filed   ☐ estimated, a 1992 tax return **will not** be filed

	Total 1992	Estimated 1993
a. Wages, salaries, tips, and other compensation		
(1) Student's parent	$_____.00	$_____.00
(2) Parent's current spouse	$_____.00	$_____.00
b. Interest income	$_____.00	$_____.00
c. Dividends	$_____.00	$_____.00
d. Net income (or loss) from business or farm. If negative, enter amount in (parentheses)	$_____.00	$_____.00
For questions 9e and 9f, list kinds and amounts in Section V, "Remarks."		
e. All other taxable income	$_____.00	$_____.00
f. Adjustments to income	$_____.00	$_____.00

Section III — Parent's (and Current Spouse's) Annual Income and Expenses (continued)

		Total 1992	Estimated 1993
10.	Total **nontaxable income** (See instructions.)		
	a. Untaxed social security benefits	$_____.00	$_____.00
	b. All other income—child support received, welfare benefits, veterans benefits, housing allowances, etc. (List kinds and amounts in Section V, "Remarks.")	$_____.00	$_____.00

Expenses (See instructions.)

		Total 1992			Total 1992
11.	U.S. income tax paid	$_____.00	**14.** Medical and dental expenses not paid by insurance	$_____.00
12.	IRS itemized deductions, if applicable	$_____.00	**15.** Other unusual expenses (List kinds and amounts in Section V, "Remarks.")	$_____.00
13.	State and local taxes	$_____.00		

Section IV — Parent's (and Current Spouse's) Assets and Debts

16. **a.** Housing payment (Check one.) ☐ rent ☐ mortgage   **b.** Monthly amount (If zero, explain in Section V, "Remarks.") $_____.00

		Year purchased	Purchase price	Present market value	Unpaid mortgage principal
17.	Home—if owned or being purchased	_____	$_____.00	$_____.00	$_____.00
18.	Other real estate	_____	$_____.00	$_____.00	$_____.00
19.	Cash, savings, checking accounts, and bonds			$_____.00	
20.	Investments—net value of stocks and other securities (List kinds and amounts in Section V, "Remarks.")			$_____.00	
21.	Business and/or farm	**a.** Present market value		$_____.00	
		b. Indebtedness		$_____.00	
		c. Percent of ownership		_____%	
22.	Other debts outstanding (Do **not** include any debts entered above. List kinds, purposes, and amounts in Section V, "Remarks.")			$_____.00	

Section V — Remarks

Section VI — Certification and Authorization

I declare that the information reported on this form is true, correct, and complete.

I agree that, to verify information reported on this form, I will on request provide an official copy of my state or U.S. income tax return.

I further agree to provide, if requested, any other official documentation necessary to verify information reported.

Student applicant's parent's signature

_____

Date completed_____

▶ Do you authorize the college to discuss the information outlined on this form with the student applicant?

yes ☐   no ☐

21423-01582 • S82M120 • 236194 • Printed in U.S.A.

Another question which appears on the FAF form is, "Is there an agreement specifying a contribution for the student's education?"

You may have a written agreement in your divorce or separation that your ex-spouse is going to help support you and your children with the cost of their education. However, if your spouse does not abide by this agreement, why should the custodial parent be penalized? In many cases the courts can't even get these non-custodial parents to come up with money that's been promised for years. So, if you have an agreement and your ex-spouse is not going to honor that agreement, in reality, you have no agreement at all.

Sometimes an ex-spouse *will agree* to pay for *half* of the children's college education. When this agreement is made, one parent may have a state or community college in mind with a total cost of $3,000 to $9,000, while the other parent is thinking of a private school with a total cost of $24,000 per year. The bottom line is don't rely on any agreement unless you receive the cost of the child's education from your ex, up front.

Divorced/Separated Parent's Statement

Although the federal formula for financial aid does not include financial information for the non-custodial parent, many colleges still want this information. These colleges will send a copy of the Divorced/Separated Parent's Statement to the custodial parent, to send on to the non-custodial parent. Even if the non-custodial parent refuses to contribute to the child's college education, the college will still use this information to justify a decrease in your financial aid eligibility. Unless your ex-mate is very poor, many custodial parents write a letter to the school confirming that they have sent the application on to their ex, explaining that the ex-mate is uncooperative and unlikely to fill out and return the application. Then they promptly throw the Divorced/Separated Parent's Statement into the trash can. I'm not saying that this is what you should do, but it has proven to be a way for many families to maintain high eligibility for financial aid dictated by the federal formula.

The following is a copy of the Divorced/Separated Parent's Statement.

CASE STUDY #3

The Spectors have been separated for seven years and divorced for three years. Marsha Spector is supposed to receive child support, however, her ex-husband hasn't sent any money in the last two years. Even though it was written into their divorce agreement that they would split the cost of college for their daughter Connie, he now says that he had a state college in mind when he agreed to splitting the cost. Since the cost of the state school was $6,000, he was prepared to come up with $3,000 per year in college costs and not one cent more.

Marsha was devastated. The thought that she might not be able to send Connie to the college of her dreams was breaking her heart. Connie was her only daughter and a gifted child. She couldn't bear to compromise her child's education because of this misunderstanding. So Marsha got some good advice from a college financial aid consultant and proceeded to have Connie apply to the finest and most expensive colleges in the country.

Now Connie is in her third year at the college of her dreams. Connie's financial aid package reflected Marsha's income and assets without those of her ex-husband. Marsha told the colleges that there was no contact with her ex-husband and even showed them court papers showing that she was suing him for back child support. She also showed them a letter from her lawyer saying that he wasn't very optimistic about collecting the back child support and that most likely Marsha would never see a penny of that money. The college eventually gave Marsha and Connie an $18,500 financial aid package so Marsha had to pay only $5,500 per year to meet the total cost of college which was $23,000 per year. Marsha did receive $3,000 from her ex-husband the first year, but she hasn't heard from him since. Connie graduates next year from an Ivy League college and Marsha is a very happy and proud mother.

A note to those thinking of remarrying

If you are thinking of remarrying and have a substantial financial aid package, or your children will be going off to college soon and you expect a substantial financial aid package based upon your income and assets, think about waiting until your youngest child is in his or her senior year of college. If you do get married, your new husband or wife's income and assets may hurt your chances of receiving financial aid. The congressional formula automatically assumes that a step-parent who lives with a custodial parent will assume all of the responsibilities of the natural parent. Even if you have a pre-nuptial agreement stating that the new spouse is *not* responsible for the educational expenses of the new step-children, the congressional formula will use the step-parent income when determining financial need.

Couples of the same gender

Some day I know that couples of the same sex who become part of a family team, whether they are raising children or not, will be entitled to the same government benefits as married couples of opposite sexes. Since the government doesn't recognize the legality of gay couples' marriages, couples of the same gender who are raising children from a previous relationship or through adoption, have the *advantage* of reporting only one parent's income and assets when it comes to applying for financial aid. They share this advantage with divorced and separated parents and unwed heterosexual couples.

Of course, being permitted to report only one parent's income and assets in a two-parent household is a great advantage and will qualify the family for a much higher dollar amount of financial aid. All couples who are co-habiting outside of marriage should be aware of this loophole and take full advantage of it.

Variable 8: Owning your own business or farm

If you have ever thought about starting your own business, the perfect time to do so is a couple of years before the children go off to college. The transfer of family cash funds to a business can substantially increase your eligibility for financial aid. If you have a business that already exists, try to hold off on as many business expenses as possible, and then take them in the base income year. It is also a good idea to take as little income as possible from the business during these base income years. By maximizing your business expenses and minimizing the amount of your income, your aid eligibility could increase tremendously. Assets

ADJUSTED NET WORTH OF A BUSINESS OR FARM

Net worth of business or farm:	Adjusted net worth:
Less than $1	$0
$1-$75,000	40% of net worth
$75,001-$225,000	$30,000 plus 50% of net worth over %75,000
$225,001-$375,000	$105,000 plus 60% of net worth over $225,000
$375,001 or more	$195,000 plus 100% of net worth over $375,000

Source: House of Representatives conference report, Higher Education Amendments of 1992.

in a business are assessed at a much lower rate than family assets. In fact, taking family assets and putting them into your business is a very good way of lowering the total amount assessed on your family's cash assets.

The table shows you that by converting *personal* assets into *business* assets, you can reduce your *assessable assets* by HALF. *That's 50%.*

Since business assets are assessed at a much lower rate than personal assets, it could be very advantageous to be able to list your real estate holdings as business assets rather than personal assets. Check with your accountant. The criteria that will determine whether or not this is legal will include how the property is used, the amount of income it produces, and whether or not you file a business tax return. Even if you meet all the legal criteria, the FAAs still have to be convinced. If they have any doubts, they will list your property as a personal asset.

The Business/Farm Supplement

If you are self employed or own your own business, some of the schools to which you are applying may ask you to fill out a **Business/Farm Supplement**. This form probes into your business net worth in greater detail than the standard FAF form. Care should be taken when filling out this form. You are being asked to list the total value of cash, receivables, inventory, and assets such as buildings and machinery. When estimating the worth of your company for the Business/Farm Supplement, make sure that you don't include "goodwill" or "location."

Variable 9: Choice of school

The ability of many parents to send a child off to an institute of higher learning will depend largely on the amount of financial aid offered by the various schools. It is for this reason that I recommend that applicants not only apply to private schools but to state, city, or community colleges where the cost of education is lower so that even if you are turned down for financial aid, the cost of attending some college will not be a problem.

Most often when we think of "safety schools" we think only of the academically safe ones— colleges where we are sure we will be accepted based on scholastic average and test scores. Just as important, however, is the "financial safety school" where, regardless of circumstances, we will be able to pay the tuition.

Some colleges are much richer than others and have more funds to *entice* prospective students to attend their institutions. These funds come from alumni and friends of the colleges in the form of scholarships or grants. When this

COLLEGE SCHOLARSHIP SERVICE
The College Board
Return this form directly to the college that provided it.

Business/Farm Supplement

Side I   School Year 1993-94

INSTRUCTIONS FOR COMPLETING THE BUSINESS/FARM SUPPLEMENT

■ If you have more than one business or farm, complete a supplement for each of them. **Return this form directly to the college, not to CSS.**

■ When completing this supplement, refer to both your 1991 and 1992 IRS tax returns — specifically, Form 1040, Schedules C, D, and F, as applicable. If an incorporated business is involved, refer to Form 1120 as well. **For any year for which tax forms have not been completed, estimate as accurately as possible.** The financial aid administrator may later ask you to provide copies of your tax returns.

■ If you are the owner or part owner of a partnership or a corporation: (1) enter your percentage of ownership (Side II, question 6); (2) enter total income, expense deductions, and profit for the entire business entity (Side I, questions 1-5); and (3) enter your share of net profit (Side I, question 6).

■ If a business is a major source of family support but no salaries are reported and business net profit is under $10,000, explain on an attached sheet how basic family expenses are met.

■ Don't submit balance sheets, profit and loss statements, cash flow statements, or tax returns in place of the Business/Farm Supplement.

■ If your home is part of the business or farm, enter its value and the amount of its mortgage on the FAF. Don't include your home value on the Business/Farm Supplement.

■ If farm income is reported on an accrual basis, the required information can be found on IRS Form 1040, Schedule F, Part III. In this case, disregard questions 1a through 1c on the Farm Supplement and begin your entries with Gross Income in question 2.

■ If you have gains or losses from the sale or exchange of livestock and/or farm machinery, report the full amount of such gains or losses in question 6 of the Farm Supplement. Don't include in this question gains or losses arising from the sale or exchange of other property, as reported on your IRS Form 1040, Schedule D.

BUSINESS OWNERS ONLY

INCOME AND EXPENSES

	1991 (Jan. 1-Dec. 31)	1992 (Jan. 1-Dec. 31)	Estimated 1993 (Jan. 1-Dec. 31)
1. BUSINESS INCOME			
a. Gross receipts or sales less returns and allowances	$	$	
b. Cost of goods sold and/or operations (Don't include salaries paid to yourself, your dependents, or others or any item listed below.)			
c. Gross profit (line 1a minus 1b)			
d. Other business income			
2. TOTAL INCOME (Add 1c and 1d.)			
3. BUSINESS DEDUCTIONS (Don't include any amount entered in 1b above.)			
a. Depreciation			
b. Interest expense			
c. Rent on business property			
d. Salaries and wages:			
1. Your salary and wages			
2. Dependents employed in the business			
Name and Relationship, Salary			
3. All other salaries and wages			
e. Other business expenses (Itemize below any item over $1,000.)			
f. Other expenses not itemized in e above			
4. TOTAL DEDUCTIONS (Add 3a-3f.)			

5. **NET PROFIT (OR LOSS):** Sole proprietor or ordinary income — Partnership or taxable income — Corporation (line 2 minus line 4).

Estimated 1993
$ _____

6. **YOUR SHARE OF LINE 5** (Multiply line 5 by your percentage of ownership, question 6 on Side II.)

1991	1992	Estimated 1993
$	$	$

7. **BUSINESS-RELATED CAPITAL GAINS (or losses)** (from Form 1040, Schedule D)

1991	1992
$	$

8. Your share of line 7. (Multiply line 7 by your percentage of ownership, question 6 on Side II.)

$	$

FARM OWNERS ONLY

INCOME AND EXPENSES

The IRS line references are for 1991. For 1992, use the corresponding lines from 1992 IRS forms.

	1991 (Jan. 1-Dec. 31)	1992 (Jan. 1-Dec. 31)	Estimated 1993 (Jan. 1-Dec. 31)
1. FARM INCOME			
a. Profit (or loss) on sales of livestock and other items purchased for resale (from Form 1040, Schedule F, line 3)	$	$	
b. Sales of livestock and produce raised (from Schedule F, line 4)			
c. Other farm income (from Schedule F, lines 5b, 6b, 7a, 7c, 8b, 8d, 9, 10)			
2. GROSS INCOME (Add 1a-1c.) (from Schedule F, line 11)			
3. FARM EXPENSES			
a. Farm deductions less depreciation (from Schedule F, lines 12-16 and lines 18-35)			
b. Depreciation (from Schedule F, line 17)			
4. TOTAL EXPENSES (Add 3a and 3b.) (from Schedule F, line 36)			
5. NET FARM PROFIT (OR LOSS) (line 2 minus line 4) (from Schedule F, line 37)			
6. FARM-RELATED CAPITAL GAINS (or losses) from sale or exchange of livestock and farm machinery (from Form 1040, Schedule D)			

7. **TOTAL FARM NET PROFIT** (Add lines 5 and 6.)

Estimated 1993
$ _____

8. **YOUR SHARE NET PROFIT** (Multiply line 7 by your percentage of ownership, question 6 on Side II.)

		Estimated 1993
$	$	$

STUDENT'S NAME:

LAST	FIRST

STUDENT'S YEAR IN COLLEGE
☐ 1st   ☐ 3rd   ☐ 5th or more
☐ 2nd   ☐ 4th   ☐ Graduate/professional

21423-01600 · Y82M140 · 236285

COLLEGE SCHOLARSHIP SERVICE
The College Board
Return this form directly to the college that provided it.

Business/Farm Supplement
Side II

School Year 1993-94

STUDENT'S INFORMATION

STUDENT'S NAME										MONTH	DAY	YEAR
	LAST NAME		FIRST NAME	MID. INIT.		SOCIAL SECURITY NO.				DATE OF BIRTH		

STUDENT'S ADDRESS				
	STREET ADDRESS	CITY	STATE	ZIP CODE

BUSINESS/FARM INFORMATION

1. NAME OF BUSINESS/FARM

2. DATE BUSINESS COMMENCED OR FARM PURCHASED: MONTH DAY YEAR

3. LOCATION OF BUSINESS/FARM
STREET ADDRESS — CITY/TOWNSHIP — COUNTY — STATE — ZIP CODE

4. TYPE OF BUSINESS/FARM
☐ Sole proprietor   ☐ Corporation
☐ Partnership   Indicate type _____

5. IF PARTNERSHIP, give name(s) of partners and their percentage of ownership.

6. YOUR PERCENTAGE OF OWNERSHIP _____ %

7. NUMBER OF EMPLOYEES _____

8. DESCRIBE PRINCIPAL PRODUCT OR SERVICE.

9. RESIDENCE INFORMATION:

Farm owners: Do you live on the farm?   ☐ Yes ☐ No

Business owners:

Is the business a part of your home?   ☐ Yes ☐ No

If yes, what percentage of home is claimed for business use? _____ %

10.

	TOTAL ACRES OWNED			
	Market value per acre	No. of acres owned	No. rented from others	No. rented to others
Tillable land				
Non-tillable land				
Woodlands and waste				
Agricultural reserve				
TOTAL				

ASSETS

11. CURRENT ASSETS	As of: 12/31/91	As of: 12/31/92
a. Cash	$	$
b. Short-term investments		
c. Receivables (net of reserve for bad debts)		
d. Inventories (Include hay, grain, livestock, and other farm products.)		
e. Other current assets not included above		
f. Total current assets (Add 11a-11e.)		
12. FIXED ASSETS (Current market value)		
a. Land and buildings (Don't include home.)		
b. Machinery and equipment		
c. Other fixed assets		
d. Total fixed assets (Add 12a-12c.)		
13. OTHER ASSETS		
a. Loans to partner(s) or stockholder(s)		
b. Other loans		
c. Investments		
d. All other assets		
e. Total other assets (Add 13a-13d.)		
14. TOTAL ASSETS (Add 11f, 12d, and 13e.)		
15. MULTIPLY TOTAL ASSETS BY PERCENTAGE OF OWNERSHIP.	$	$

INDEBTEDNESS

16. CURRENT DEBTS	As of: 12/31/91	As of: 12/31/92
a. Accounts payable	$	$
b. Other current debts		
c. Total current debts (Add 16a and 16b.)		
17. LONG-TERM DEBTS (Don't include any amount listed above.)		
a. Mortgages on land and buildings (Don't include home mortgages.)		
b. Debts secured by equipment		
c. Loans from partner(s) or stockholder(s)		
d. Other debts		
e. Total long-term debts (Add 17a-17d.)		
18. TOTAL INDEBTEDNESS (Add 16c and 17e.)		
19. MULTIPLY TOTAL INDEBTEDNESS BY PERCENTAGE OF OWNERSHIP.	$	$

SIGNATURES

FATHER'S OR STEPFATHER'S SIGNATURE — DATE

MOTHER'S OR STEPMOTHER'S SIGNATURE — DATE

money is combined with state and federal funds, it gives wealthy colleges the ability to offer more generous financial aid packages than the colleges with whom they are competing. However, the colleges that are the wealthiest are usually also the finest colleges in the country and certainly don't have to worry about giving generous financial aid packages in order to attract desirable applicants. When these colleges are competing with each other for a "super desirable" student, however, it is often the college with the most generous financial aid package that wins the prized student.

When it comes to exceptionally bright students, most colleges are willing to give some sort of academic scholarship as an incentive whether or not there is sufficient need. Landing an exceptionally bright student also allows the school to accept a below average student without lowering the school's overall average.

Again, your children should always be encouraged to apply to their first choice in colleges regardless of that college's cost.

Apply to at least six colleges

Aside from being assured that you will have a college that has accepted you, applying to many schools has another purpose. Being able to compare the financial aid packages of various schools gives you the ability to evaluate, compare, and even negotiate the best college buy. At a time when colleges are bidding for students in order to survive the drop in college applications (due to the drop in the birth rate 17 years ago), it is in the applicant's interest to apply to many colleges. Since the colleges are aware of the other colleges that you are applying to (this information is given to the colleges by the needs analysis services) they know that a large financial incentive (a college grant) can make the difference in choosing their college. The news will arrive in the form of a **Financial Award Letter**. The letter will tell you the cost of education at the college and just how much of it your family will have to come up with.

Final tips

Now that you have a better understanding about how the college financial aid system works and how you can increase the amount of your financial aid, here are some final tips.

Contact the financial aid administrator at each school you're interested in. He or she can tell you what aid programs are available there, and how much the total cost of education will be. If you're in high school, also talk to your guidance counselor. He or she can tell you about financial aid in general and where to look for help.

Ask the state higher education agency in your home state for information about state aid — including aid from a program jointly funded by individual states and the U.S. Department of Education. Each state has its own name for this program, as well as its own award levels, eligibility criteria, and application procedures.

Find out about financial aid

You have the right to ask the school the following:

- What financial assistance is available, including information on all federal, state, local, private, and institutional financial aid programs. You also have the right to know how a school selects financial aid recipients.
- What the procedures and deadlines are for submitting applications for each available financial aid program.
- How the school determines your financial need. This process includes how costs for tuition and fees, room and board, travel, books and supplies, and personal and miscellaneous expenses are considered in your cost of education. It also includes the resources considered in calculating your need (such as parental contribution, other financial aid, assets, etc.). You also have the right to know how much of your financial need— as determined by the school— has been met, and how and when you'll receive your aid.
- How the school determines the types and amount of assistance in your financial aid package. You also have the right to ask the school to reconsider your aid package if you believe a mistake has been made, or if your enrollment or financial circumstances have changed.
- How the school determines whether you're making satisfactory academic progress, and what happens if you're not. Whether you continue to receive federal financial aid depends, in part, on whether you're making satisfactory progress.
- What the interest rate is on any student loan you may receive, the total amount you must repay, the length of time you have to repay, when you must start repaying, and what cancellation or **deferment** (postponement) provisions apply.

- If you're offered a College Work-Study job — what kind of job it is, what hours you must work, what your duties will be, what the rate of pay will be, and how and when you'll be paid.
- Who the school's financial aid personnel are, where they're located, and how to contact them for information.

Understand your school's refund policy

You have the right to know what your school's policy is. If something happens and you never register for classes, or if you drop out of school within a short time after you start, you may be able to get part of your educational expenses returned to you. But after a certain date, you won't get any money back. Check with your school to find out what expenses you may have to pay if you drop out. Keep in mind that if you receive federal student aid from any of the programs mentioned — other than College Work-Study — some or all of that aid will be returned to those programs or to your lender.

The school must explain its refund policy, in writing, to all students— prospective as well as current. For specific information about the **refund policy** at your school, contact your financial aid administrator.

Check several sources to find out the answers to questions you may have about a school

Talk to high school counselors, local employers, and the state Department of Education that has jurisdiction over the school. See if any complaints about the school have been filed with the local Better Business Bureau, Chamber of Commerce, or consumer protection division of the state Attorney General's office. And contact these organizations if you have a complaint about a school.

Remember, colleges are businesses. Shop around and negotiate to get the best buy.

Records needed

When you fill out an application you should have certain records on hand.

The most recent U.S. income tax return is the most important record, since you must use specific numbers from specific lines on the tax return to fill out your application. You'll need to refer to:

- your tax return,
- your parent's return (if you apply as a dependent student), and
- your spouse's return (if you're married and your spouse filed a separate return).

Referring to the tax form will make it easier for you to complete your application and get it through the processing system.

You may apply even if the tax return is not yet completed. However, this means you'll have to estimate the financial information on your application, and you may have to prove the accuracy of your estimate before you're awarded aid. Also, you'll have to change later any figures that prove to be incorrect.

Other useful records to have on hand

- W-2 forms and other records of income received.
- Current bank statements and mortgage information.
- Records of benefits received from the Social Security Administration, Department of Veterans' Affairs, and other agencies.

You should save all records and all other materials used to prepare your application because you'll need them later if either the U.S. Department of Education or your school selects you for a process called **validation**. This means *you'll have to prove that what you report on your application is correct.* (Many schools require *all* financial aid applicants to verify the information they report.) As part of the validation process, you'll have to give your financial aid administrator certain information or documents, such as the ones mentioned in this section. If you don't provide proof, you won't receive aid from the U.S. Department of Education, and you may not receive aid from other sources. So make sure you keep the documents mentioned, and make sure the information you report is accurate!

Note: Aid from federal programs is not guaranteed from one year to the next. You must re-apply every year. Also, if you change schools, your aid doesn't necessarily go with you. Check with your new school to find out what steps you must take.

4. OBTAINING STATE AID

When you fill out your federal financial aid forms, you will also answer questions pertaining to state aid. Often, there is a terrific financial advantage if you attend college in the state in which you reside. Many states give grants, loans, and tuition reductions to state residents.

As soon as this information is learned by many high school students, their minds start churning and scheming about how they will become a resident of the state where they want to go to school and save themselves and their families thousands of dollars. They don't realize that establishing residency will also require that they establish independence from their parents. After all, it's difficult to be a resident of one state and be dependent on your parents who are residents of another state. I'm not saying that it can't be done. What I am saying is that it takes long-term planning to establish both student independence and residency unless your parents also plan to move to the state where you will be attending college.

Establishing **residency** in another state for the purpose of reducing college costs can also be considered fraud. Factors such as length of time in state, employment and sources of financial support, payment of state taxes, and voting records are all taken into account. At colleges in many states, you can meet all of the qualifications and still be turned down if the college feels that your residency is simply a ploy to reduce college costs.

The states that give the most financial aid to residents are New York, New Jersey, Pennsylvania, California, and Illinois. To find out what programs are available in your state, write to your state's Department of Education.

Note: even if you are eligible for state aid, sometimes it can still cost you less to attend an out-of-state school. Many colleges looking for exceptional students from various parts of the country can give you a financial incentive bigger than your state. If you feel you can't afford to send your children to an out-of-state school, apply anyway. It could end up costing you less.

State aid consists of grants and loans based upon need and/or merit, given to students attending public and private colleges within their own state. Although all 50 states award financial aid based on "need," the criteria used to determine that "need" can differ from state to state. For instance, in New York state, the eligibility for aid is determined by the amount of your family's taxable state income. You can have a million dollars in assets in New York state and still get financial aid. Some states have reciprocal agreements with other states to let students attend the other state's colleges and still retain their home-state financial aid. Rules differ from state to state.

How to apply for state aid

In December of your child's senior year in high school, the guidance office will distribute Financial Aid and Needs Analysis Forms. Some states have their own versions of this form which incorporate state aid with the Financial Aid Form for federal aid. In states where these forms are separate, you will receive a supplementary state form along with the federal form. If your high school does not have the state form, call your state Department of Education to request one. If you are eligible for state aid, the type and amount will be listed on the college's financial aid package which you will receive when the college accepts you. Sometimes the amount of state aid at different colleges within the same state may vary. This is usually due to differences in the cost of tuition. If the cost of the colleges is about the same, the amount of state financial aid should be about the same.

5. FORMS

Most students apply for financial aid by filling out one or more of the forms listed below. Your school may specify which of the forms listed below you should complete. Your school will have the form you need. The forms are:

Free Application for Federal Student Aid (FAFSA)
College Scholarship Service's 66
Financial Aid Form (FAF)
Student Loan Application

If you want to apply for federal aid only, fill out only the FAFSA form. It's free. The following pages will give you an idea of what the latest forms look like.

The various companies that process these forms are referred to as financial aid analysis services (formally known as needs analysis services). The two most popular are the **CSS (College Scholarship Service)** and **ACT (American College Testing)**. These companies process the family financial aid information and send the results on to the colleges, the state, and back to you.

In the past, these services also informed the colleges with whom they were competing for a student's attendance. This allowed the colleges to fix their financial aid awards, as detailed in the previous chapter. However, this situation no longer exists. Now, there is open bidding for students. Knowledge of the competition can have a very positive affect on the size and the sources of your financial aid package. If a college wants to lure a student away from a competitive college, the financial aid officer will offer as much incentive as possible, especially if the application is from a "desirable" student. The following is a copy of the College Scholarship Service's FAF form, the Free Application for Federal Student Aid (FAFSA), and the Student Loan Application Form.

Section E (to be completed by student)

SKIDMORE COLLEGE STATEMENT OF UNDERSTANDING

All students applying for any type of student aid must read and sign the following:

I certify that the information on this application is true to the best of my knowledge at this time. I agree to file an accurate 1993-94 Financial Aid Form by the required Skidmore deadline and will provide a copy of my own 1992 U.S. Federal Tax Return, with all pages, schedules, and W-2 forms or their equivalent (non-taxable income sources statement), as soon as they are available.

I understand the responsibilities incurred by this application (as outlined in the instructions enclosed with this application) and agree to provide additional information that may be necessary for the evaluation of my application and/or for continuing my eligibility for any financial assistance program(s) administered by Skidmore. In addition, I agree to send immediate notice of any change in information to Skidmore, including the receipt of other scholarships or grants not previously reported.

I authorize Skidmore Student Aid staff to discuss my application with other colleges, donors, agencies, or organizations that may also be considering me for aid. To assist in determining financial need, I authorize the Student Aid staff to discuss the information contained in my application materials and the Financial Aid Form with my parents.

Student's Signature _____ Date _____

STUDENT STATEMENT OF EDUCATIONAL PURPOSE

I will use all Title IV money received — Pell, SEOG, Perkins Loan (formerly NDSL), CWSP, Stafford Student Loan (formerly GSL), PLUS and SLS — only for expenses related to my study at Skidmore College. I understand that I am responsible for repaying any funds I receive that cannot reasonably be attributed to meeting my educational expenses at Skidmore College.

I certify that I do not owe a refund on any grant, am not in default on any loan, and have not borrowed in excess of the loan limits under Title IV programs, at any institution. I am also aware that in order to continue to receive assistance from any Title IV programs, I must maintain satisfactory progress in the course of study I am pursuing according to the standards and practices of Skidmore College.

STUDENT STATEMENT OF REGISTRATION STATUS

_____ I certify that I am registered with the Selective Service.

_____ I certify that I am not required to be registered with the Selective Service, because:

    _____ I am female.

    _____ I am in the armed services on active duty.
    (Note: Does not apply to members of the Reserves and National Guard who are not on active duty.)

    _____ I have not reached my 18th birthday.

    _____ I was born before 1960.

    _____ I am a citizen of the Federated States of Micronesia, the Marshall Islands,
    or a permanent resident of the Trust Territory of the Pacific Islands (Palau).

STUDENT ANTI-DRUG ABUSE ACT CERTIFICATION

_____ I certify that, as a condition of my Pell Grant, I will not engage in the unlawful manufacture, distribution, dispensation, possession, or use of a controlled substance during the period covered by my Pell Grant.

I declare under penalty of perjury that the foregoing is true and correct.

Student's Signature _____ Date _____

(These statements cover the period of July 1, 1993 to June 30, 1994.)

OPTIONAL

_____ I grant permission and request that routine copies of my student aid and amended awards be sent (first-class U.S. mail) to the address of my parent of record (address within Skidmore College data system) when I am on campus during the academic year.

Student's Signature _____ Date _____

Section D: 1992 Income, Earnings, and Benefits

*(You **must** see the instructions for income and taxes that you should exclude from questions 19 through 23.)*

17. The following 1992 U.S. income tax figures are from...

Everyone must fill out the Student (& Spouse) column below.

PARENTS
(Check only one box.)

1. ☐ a completed 1992 IRS Form 1040A or 1040EZ. (Go to 18.)
2. ☐ a completed 1992 IRS Form 1040. (Go to 18.)
3. ☐ an estimated 1992 IRS Form 1040A or 1040EZ. (Go to 18.)
4. ☐ an estimated 1992 IRS Form 1040. (Go to 18.)
5. ☐ A tax return will not be filed. (Skip to 21.)

STUDENT (& SPOUSE)
(Check only one box.)

1. ☐ a completed 1992 IRS Form 1040A or 1040EZ. (Go to 18.)
2. ☐ a completed 1992 IRS Form 1040. (Go to 18.)
3. ☐ an estimated 1992 IRS Form 1040A or 1040EZ. (Go to 18.)
4. ☐ an estimated 1992 IRS Form 1040. (Go to 18.)
5. ☐ A tax return will not be filed. (Skip to 21.)

TAX FILERS ONLY

18. 1992 Total number of exemptions (Form 1040-line 6e, or 1040A-line 6e; 1040EZ filers, see instructions on pages 4 and 5) |__|__|

19. 1992 Adjusted Gross Income (AGI)–Form 1040-line 31, 1040A-line 16, or 1040EZ-line 3, or see instructions on page 5. $_____.00

20. 1992 U.S. income tax paid (Form 1040-line 46, 1040A-line 25, or 1040EZ-line 7) $_____.00

21. 1992 Income earned from work   Father $_____.00

22. 1992 Income earned from work   Mother $_____.00

TAX FILERS ONLY

18. |__|__|

19. $_____.00

20. $_____.00

Student **21.** $_____.00

Spouse **22.** $_____.00

23. 1992 Untaxed income and benefits *(yearly totals only)*

23a. Social security benefits $_____.00   **23a.** $_____.00

23b. Aid to Families with Dependent Children (AFDC or ADC) $_____.00   **23b.** $_____.00

23c. Child support received for all children $_____.00   **23c.** $_____.00

23d. Other untaxed income and benefits from Worksheet #2 on page 11. $_____.00   **23d.** $_____.00

Section E: Federal Stafford Loan Information (Formerly Guaranteed Student Loan [GSL])

If you have never received a Stafford Loan (GSL) or a Federal Insured Student Loan (FISL), go to question 29. Skip questions 24 through 28.

24. What is the total unpaid principal balance on **all** your Stafford Loans (GSLs)? $_____.00
(If you answered "0," go to question 29. Skip questions 25 through 28.)

25. What is the unpaid principal balance on your **most recent** Stafford Loan (GSL)? $_____.00

26. What is the interest rate of your **most recent** Stafford Loan (GSL)?   1 ☐ 7%   2 ☐ 8%   3 ☐ 9%   4 ☐ 8%/10%   5 ☐ Variable Rate

27. What was the loan period of your **most recent** Stafford Loan (GSL)?   from |__|__|__|__| through |__|__|__|__|
Month Year   Month Year

28. What was your class level when you received your **most recent** Stafford Loan (GSL)?
(Check only one box.)

1. ☐ Freshman
2. ☐ Sophomore
3. ☐ Junior
4. ☐ Senior
5. ☐ 5th year or more undergraduate
6. ☐ 1st year graduate or professional (beyond a Bachelor's degree)
7. ☐ Continuing graduate or professional

29. What is your permanent home telephone number? |__|__|__|__|__|__|__|__|__|__|
Area Code

30. What is your driver's license number? *(Be sure to include the abbreviation of the State that issued it.)* |__|__|__|__|__|__|__|__|__|__|__|__|__|__|__|__|__|__|__|__|__|
State

Section F: Your Veterans Education Benefits Per Month
(for the student only)

31. Your veterans education benefits
(See the instructions on page 6.)

31a. Amount per month $_____.00

31b. Number of months |__|__| months

Section G: College Release and Certification

32. What college(s) do you plan to attend in 1993-94?   *(**Note:** By answering this question, you are giving permission to send your application data to the college(s) you list below.)*

	College Name	Street Address	City	State
32a.				
32b.				
32c.				
32d.				
32e.				
32f.				

33. Do you give the U.S. Department of Education permission to send information from this form to the financial aid agencies in your State as well as to the State agencies of any college listed in question 32?

❑ Yes   ❑ No

34. ❑ Check this box if you give Selective Service permission to register you. *(See the instructions on page 7.)*

> **Note:** Contact the financial aid administrator at your school if:
> - your family has tuition expenses at an elementary or secondary school,
> - your family has unusual medical or dental expenses, not covered by insurance,
> - a member of your family is a dislocated worker, or
> - you have unusual circumstances not covered in this form that would affect your eligibility for student financial aid.

School Use Only

Dependency
Override: enter D or I |__|

Title IV Inst.
Number |__|__|__|__|__|__|

FAA Signature: _____

Dept. of Ed Use Only
(Do not write in this box.) |__|__|__|__|__|__|__|

35. Read and sign

Certification: All of the information provided by me or any other person on this form and the Supplemental Information (Sections H and I), if completed, is true and complete to the best of my knowledge. I understand that this application is being filed jointly by all signatories. If asked by an authorized official, I agree to give proof of the information that I have given on this form and the Supplemental Information (Sections H and I), if completed. I realize that this proof may include a copy of my U.S., State, or local income tax return. I also realize that if I do not give proof when asked, the student may be denied aid.

I certify that I, the student, do not owe a refund on any Federal student grant, am not in default on any Federal student loan, and have not borrowed in excess of the Federal student loan limits, under the Federal student aid programs, at any institution.

Everyone giving information on this form must sign below. If you don't sign this form, it will be returned unprocessed.

1 Student _____

2 Student's spouse _____

3 Father (Stepfather) _____

4 Mother (Stepmother) _____

Date completed |__|__|__|__| Year   ❑ 1993
Month   Day   ❑ 1994

Preparer's Use Only   *(Students and parents: don't fill out this section.)*

36a. Preparer's Name |__|__|__|__|__|__|__|__|__|__|__|__|__|__|__|__|__| |__|__|__|__|__|__|__|__|__| |__|
Last   First   M.I.

36b. Firm's Name and Address
(or yours if self-employed) |__|__|__|__|__|__|__|__|__|__|__|__|__|__|__|__|__|__|__|__|__|__|__|__|__|__|
Firm Name

|__|__|__|__|__|__|__|__|__|__|__|__|__|__|__|__|__|__|__|__|__|__|__|__|__|__|
Number and Street (Include Apt. No.)

|__|__|__|__|__|__|__|__|__|__|__|__|__|__|__|__|__|__| |__|__| |__|__|__|__|__|
City   State   ZIP Code

36c. Employer Identification Number (EIN) |__|__|__|__|__|__|__|__|__|

36d. Preparer's social security number |__|__|__|__|__|__|__|__|__|

36e. Certification: All of the information on this form and the Supplemental Information (Sections H and I) if completed, is true and complete to the best of my knowledge.

Preparer's Signature _____   Date _____/_____/_____

If you are filling out the GREEN and WHITE areas, go to page 7 and complete WORKSHEET A. This will tell you whether you must fill out Sections H and I. You may be able to skip Section H, if you meet certain tax filing and income conditions.

If you are filling out the GRAY and WHITE areas, go to page 7 and complete WORKSHEET B. This will tell you whether you must fill out Sections H and I. You may be able to skip Section H, if you meet certain tax filing and income conditions.

———*Supplemental Information* ———

Section H: Asset Information

	PARENTS		**STUDENT (& SPOUSE)**	
37. Write in the age of your older parent.	⌷ ⌷ ⌷		37. XXXXXXXXXX	
	What is it worth today?	**What is owed on it?**	**What is it worth today?**	**What is owed on it?**
38. Cash, savings, and checking accounts	$_____.00	XXXXXXXXXX	38. $_____.00	XXXXXXXXXX
39. Other real estate and investments *(Don't include the home.)*	$_____.00	$_____.00	39. $_____.00	$_____.00
40. Business	$_____.00	$_____.00	40. $_____.00	$_____.00
41. Farm	$_____.00	$_____.00	41. $_____.00	$_____.00
42. Is the family living on the farm?	☐ Yes ☐ No		42. ☐ Yes ☐ No	

STOP

If you are applying for Federal aid, you must complete questions 45b, 45e, 46, and 47 below. You **may** need to fill out **ALL OF** Section I, below, if you are applying for State or college aid. Check with your financial aid administrator. If you are not required to fill out Section I, you have finished the application. Recheck your application. **MAKE SURE THAT YOU HAVE COMPLETED SECTION G. Mail the application to:** Federal Student Aid Programs, P.O. Box 6376, Princeton, NJ 08541.

Section I: State Information *(Fill out this section if you are applying for State aid. Your school may also require you to fill out this section. Also, your State or school may require additional information. If you are required to fill out this section, be sure to see the deadline dates under "Deadline for State Student Aid" on page 10. Check with your financial aid administrator.)*

43. a. What is the highest grade level your father completed? *(Check only one box.)*

₁ ☐ elementary school (K-8) ₃ ☐ college or beyond

₂ ☐ high school (9-12) ₄ ☐ unknown

b. What is the highest grade level your mother completed? *(Check only one box.)*

₁ ☐ elementary school (K-8) ₃ ☐ college or beyond

₂ ☐ high school (9-12) ₄ ☐ unknown

44. If you (the student) did or will receive your high school diploma by...

graduating from high school, give the date here:

⌷ ⌷ ■ ⌷ ⌷
Month   Year

-OR-

earning a GED, give the date here:

⌷ ■ ⌷ ⌷
Month   Year

45a. If you are (or were) in college, do you plan to attend *that same college* in 1993-94? ☐ Yes ☐ No

45b. What will be your enrollment status during the 1993-94 school year?

School Term	Full Time	3/4 Time	1/2 Time	Less Than 1/2 Time	Not Enrolled
		(Check only one enrollment status for each term that applies.)			
Summer '93	₁ ☐	₂ ☐	₃ ☐	₄ ☐	₅ ☐
Fall '93	₁ ☐	₂ ☐	₃ ☐	₄ ☐	₅ ☐
Winter '94	₁ ☐	₂ ☐	₃ ☐	₄ ☐	₅ ☐
Spring '94	₁ ☐	₂ ☐	₃ ☐	₄ ☐	₅ ☐

45c. What will be your degree/certificate and course of study? *(See the instructions on page 9.)*

⌷ ⌷ ⌷ - ⌷ ⌷ ⌷ ⌷
Degree/Cert.   Course of Study

45d. When do you expect to complete your degree/certificate?

⌷ ⌷ ⌷ ⌷
Month   Year

45e. What will be your year in college during the 1993-94 school year? *(Check only one box.)*

₁ ☐ 1st ₃ ☐ 3rd ₅ ☐ 5th year or more undergraduate

₂ ☐ 2nd ₄ ☐ 4th ₆ ☐ graduate

46. What will be your housing status?

₁ ☐ Campus housing ₂ ☐ Off-campus ₃ ☐ With parents/relatives

47. For how many dependent children will you pay child care expenses in 1993-94? ⌷ ⌷

Section A — Student's Identification Information – Be sure to complete this section. Answer the questions the same way you answered them in Section A of the Free Application for Federal Student Aid (FAFSA).

1. Your name

Last   First   M.I.

3. Title (optional)

1 ☐ Mr.   2 ☐ Miss, Ms., or Mrs.

2. Your permanent mailing address
(Mail will be sent to this address.)

Number, street, and apartment number

City   State   Zip Code

4. Your date of birth

Month   Day   Year

5. Your social security number

☐☐☐–☐☐–☐☐☐☐

Section B — Student's Other Information

6. If you are now in high school, give your high school 6-digit code number.

7. What year will you be in college in 1993-94? (Mark only one box.)

1 ☐ 1st (never previously attended college)
2 ☐ 1st (previously attended college)
3 ☐ 2nd
4 ☐ 3rd
5 ☐ 4th
6 ☐ 5th or more undergraduate
7 ☐ first-year graduate/professional (beyond a bachelor's degree)
8 ☐ second-year graduate/professional
9 ☐ third-year graduate/professional
0 ☐ fourth-year or more graduate/professional

8. a. If you have previously attended any college or other postsecondary school, write in the total number of colleges and schools you have attended. ☐

b. List below the colleges (up to five) that you have attended. Begin with the college you attended most recently. Use the CSS code numbers from the list in the FAF instruction booklet. If more space is needed, use Section M.

Name, city, and state of college	Period of attendance From (mo./yr.)	To (mo./yr.)	CSS Code Number

9. During the 1993-94 school year, you want institutional financial aid

from ☐☐ ☐☐   through ☐☐ ☐☐
Month Year   Month Year

10. Mark your preference for institutional work and/or loan assistance.

1 ☐ Part-time job only
2 ☐ Loan only
3 ☐ Will accept both, but prefer loan
4 ☐ Will accept both, but prefer job
5 ☐ No preference

11. If it is necessary to borrow money to pay for educational expenses, do you want to be considered for a Stafford Loan? (optional)

Yes ☐ 1   No ☐ 2

(If you mark "Yes," your information may be sent to the loan agency within your state.)

12. a. Your employer/occupation _____

b. Employer's address _____

c. Will you continue to work for this employer during the 1993-94 school year? Yes ☐ 1 No ☐ 2

13. If you have dependents other than a spouse, how many will be in each of the following age groups during 1993-94?

Ages 0-5 ☐   Ages 6-12 ☐   Ages 13+ ☐

14. 1992 child support paid by you $_____.00

Section C — Student's Expected Summer/School-Year Income

	Summer 1993 3 months	School Year 1993-94 9 months		Summer 1993 3 months	School Year 1993-94 9 months
15. Income earned from work by you	$_____.00	$_____.00	**17.** Other taxable income	$_____.00	$_____.00
16. Income earned from work by spouse	$_____.00	$_____.00	**18.** Nontaxable income and benefits	$_____.00	$_____.00

Print your name   Last |⎵|⎵|⎵|⎵|⎵|⎵|⎵|⎵|⎵|⎵|⎵|⎵|⎵|⎵|⎵| First |⎵|⎵|⎵|⎵|⎵|⎵|⎵|

Section D — Student's (& Spouse's) Assets

What is it worth today? What is owed on it?

19. Cash and checking accounts $ _____ .00   **21. Other real estate** $ _____ .00 $ _____ .00

What is it worth today? What is owed on it?

22. Investments & savings (See instructions.) $ _____ .00 $ _____ .00

20. Home (Renters write in "0.") $ _____ .00 $ _____ .00

Section E — Family Members' Listing
Give information for all family members but don't give information about yourself. List up to seven other family members here. If there are more than seven, list first those who will be in college at least half-time. List the others in Section M.

23.

	Full name of family member / You — the Student Applicant	Age	Relationship (Use code below*)	In the 1993-94 school year, will attend college for at least one term full-time half-time	Name of school or college this person will attend in 1993-94 school year	Year in school 1993-94	If attended college in 1992-93, give amount of: 1992-93 Scholarships/Grants	1992-93 Parents' Contribution
1	You — the Student Applicant			1☐ 2☐				
2			☐	1☐ 2☐				
3			☐	1☐ 2☐				
4			☐	1☐ 2☐				
5			☐	1☐ 2☐				
6			☐	1☐ 2☐				
7			☐	1☐ 2☐				
8			☐	1☐ 2☐				

Write in the correct code from below. ↑

* **Relationship Codes:**   1 = Student's parent   3 = Student's brother/stepbrother or sister/stepsister   5 = Student's son or daughter   7 = Other (Explain in Section M.)
2 = Student's stepparent   4 = Student's husband or wife   6 = Student's grandparent

---

If you were directed to provide parents' information when you completed the Free Application for Federal Student Aid, you should also give parents' information in the following sections. Some colleges may require your parents' information even if you were not directed to provide it on the Free Application for Federal Student Aid. See page 5 of the FAF instruction booklet if you are unsure about whether you should provide parents' information.

Section F — Parents' Information — See page 5 of the FAF instruction booklet.

24. Check one: ☐ Father ☐ Stepfather ☐ Legal Guardian ☐ Other - Explain in Section M.

25. Check one: ☐ Mother ☐ Stepmother ☐ Legal Guardian ☐ Other - Explain in Section M.

a. Name _____ Age |⎵| **a.** Name _____ Age |⎵|

b. Occupation/ Employer _____ No. years _____   **b.** Occupation/ Employer _____ No. years _____

26. Parent(s) address (if different from address in question 2):   Street address: _____

City/State/Zip: _____

Section G — Divorced, Separated, or Remarried Parents
(To be answered by the parent who completes this form, if the student's natural or adoptive parents are divorced, separated, or remarried.)

27. a. Year of separation |⎵| Year of divorce |⎵|

b. Other parent's name _____
Home address _____
_____
_____
Occupation/Employer _____
_____
_____

c. According to court order, when will support for the student end? |⎵| |⎵| Month   Year

d. Who last claimed the student as a tax exemption? _____

In which year? |⎵|

e. Is there an agreement specifying a contribution for the student's education?   Yes ☐   No ☐

If yes, how much for the 1993-94 school year? $ _____ .00

Page 2

Section H — Parents' 1992 Taxable Income & Expenses

28. Breakdown of 1992 Adjusted Gross Income (AGI)

Tax Filers Only

a. Wages, salaries, tips (IRS Form 1040 — line 7, 1040A — line 7, or 1040EZ — line 1)   **28a.** $ _____ .00

b. Interest income (IRS Form 1040 — line 8a, 1040A — line 8a, or 1040EZ — line 2)   **b.** $ _____ .00

c. Dividend income (IRS Form 1040 — line 9 or 1040A — line 9)   **c.** $ _____ .00

d. Net income (or loss) from business, farm, rents, royalties, partnerships, estates, trusts, etc. (IRS Form 1040 — lines 12, 18, and 19). If a loss, enter the amount in (parentheses).   **d.** $ _____ .00

e. Other taxable income such as alimony received, capital gains (or losses), pensions, annuities, etc. (IRS Form 1040 — lines 10, 11, 13-15, 16b, 17b, 20, 21b, and 22 or 1040A — lines 10b, 11b, 12, and 13b)   **e.** $ _____ .00

f. Adjustments to income (IRS Form 1040 — line 30 or 1040A — line 15c)   **f.** $ _____ .00

29. 1992 child support paid by parent(s) completing this form.   **29.** $ _____ .00

30. 1992 medical and dental expenses not covered by insurance.   **30.** $ _____ .00

31. 1992 total elementary, junior high school, and high school tuition paid for dependent children.   **31.** $ _____ .00

Section I — Parents' 1992 Untaxed Income & Benefits

32. Write in below your other untaxed 1992 income and benefits.

a. Deductible IRA and/or Keogh payments from Form 1040, total of lines 24a, 24b, and 27 or 1040A, line 15c $ _____ .00

b. Payments to tax-deferred pension and savings plans (paid directly or withheld from earnings) Include untaxed portions of 401(k) and 403(b) plans. $ _____ .00

c. Earned income credit from Form 1040, line 56 or 1040A, line 28c $ _____ .00

d. Housing, food, and other living allowances (excluding rent subsidies for low-income housing) paid to members of the military, clergy, and others (Include cash payments and cash value of benefits.) $ _____ .00

e. Tax-exempt interest income from Form 1040, line 8b or 1040A, line 8b $ _____ .00

f. Untaxed portions of pensions from Form 1040, line 16a minus 16b and line 17a minus 17b or 1040A, line 10a minus 10b and line 11a minus 11b (excluding "rollovers") $ _____ .00

g. Foreign income exclusion from Form 2555, line 39 $ _____ .00

h. Credit for federal tax on special fuels from Form 4136–Part III: Total Income Tax Credit $ _____ .00

i. Any other untaxed income and benefits (See instructions.) $ _____ .00

Section J — Parents' 1993 Expected Income

33. 1993 income earned from work by father $ _____ .00

34. 1993 income earned from work by mother $ _____ .00

35. 1993 other taxable income $ _____ .00

36. 1993 nontaxable income and benefits $ _____ .00

Section K — Parents' Assets

37. Cash and checking accounts $ _____ .00

38. If parents own home, give

   a. year purchased | 1 | 9 | | |

   b. purchase price $ _____ .00

39. Parents' monthly home mortgage or rental payment (If none, explain in Section M.) $ _____ .00

What is it worth today?   What is owed on it?

40. Home (Renters write in "0.") $ _____ .00 $ _____ .00

41. Other real estate $ _____ .00 $ _____ .00

42. Investments & savings (See instructions.) $ _____ .00 $ _____ .00

Section L — Student's Colleges & Programs

43. List the names and CSS code numbers of up to eight colleges and programs to which you want CSS to send information from this form and from the Free Application for Federal Student Aid. Enclose the right fee. See the FAF instructions and **44**.

Name	City and State	CSS Code No.	Housing Code*

*Housing Codes for 1993-94 (Enter only one code for each college.)
1 = With parents   2 = Campus housing   3 = Off-campus housing   4 = With relatives

44. Fee: Mark the box that tells how many colleges and programs are listed in **43**.

CSS Only

1 ☐ **$9.75**   3 ☐ **$25.25**   5 ☐ **$40.75**   7 ☐ **$56.25**
2 ☐ **$17.50**   4 ☐ **$33.00**   6 ☐ **$48.50**   8 ☐ **$64.00**

Make out your check or money order for the total amount above to the College Scholarship Service. Return this form, the fee, and the Free Application for Federal Student Aid in the mailing envelope that came with your FAFSA/FAF. **You must send the correct fee with your FAF. If you fail to do so, the FAF will be returned to you unprocessed.** However, CSS will process your FAFSA without a fee.

Section M — Explanations/Special Circumstances
Use this space to explain any unusual expenses such as high medical or dental expenses, educational and other debts, or special circumstances.

Don't send letters, tax forms, or other materials with your FAF as they will be destroyed.

21701-02592 • CW122M

Certification:

All the information on this form is true and complete to the best of my knowledge. If asked by an authorized official, I agree to give proof of the information that I have given on this form. I realize that this proof may include a copy of my U.S., state, or local income tax returns. I also realize that if I don't give proof when asked, the student may not get aid. I give permission to send information from my FAFSA and FAF to the colleges and programs in **43**.

Everyone giving information on this form must sign below.

1 _____   2 _____
Student's signature   Student's spouse's signature

3 _____   4 _____
Father's (Stepfather's) signature   Mother's (Stepmother's) signature

When you have completed this form, make a copy for your records.

Date this form was completed:

| | | |
Month   Day

1 ☐ 1993
2 ☐ 1994
Year

Write in the month and day.
Mark the year completed.

☐ ☐

Page 4

Most of us are daunted by forms. In the case of applying for financial aid, they are a necessary evil. By becoming familiar with the types of forms you may be expected to fill out, you will achieve a better understanding of what each question on the form means. It will also familiarize you with which questions to watch out for. As an example, I would like to use the College Scholarship Service FAF form. Like the other financial aid service forms, it has many questions that serve as checks for other information on the form. For instance...

Question #28-b (interest income) is one of those questions. If you show $8,000 in interest income and claim only $10,000 in cash and savings, then surely a bell will go off. The financial aid administrator (FAA) at the college will surely want to know what you did with the other $150,000 you had in your savings account.

Note: $8,000 in savings interest represents over $150,000 in savings. This is why it is so important to move your savings early so there is no tax trail on your income tax form.

Question #28-c (dividend income). If you show $5,000 in dividend income, don't show investments of $10,000 (question #42) unless you're able to show proof that you have closed out most of your portfolio. In other words, tell the truth. *If you plan ahead, there is no problem with telling the truth.*

The next checkpoint is #38-a and b (What did you pay for your home and what year did you buy it?). This is the checkpoint for #40 (home value). The year and the amount that you paid for your home will be put into the computer, and the minimum value of your home will be evaluated using the government's Federal Housing Index multiplier.

If the answer to #40 (home value) is less than the answer on the Federal Housing Index multiplier, bells will be ringing. I suggest adding an additional 15% to the calculated value of your home which can be found on page 30.

There are other questions that will give the FAAs information that will allow them to use their judgment and gut feelings as to how honest you have been. Questions 24-b and 25-b ask for your parents' occupations. If Mom or Dad is a doctor or president of a corporation, having an income of $20,000 per year might look a little suspicious.

Even if all your answers coincide, chances are that when you receive your student aid report, one of the first sentences that you will see is, "Your form has been chosen for **validation**." Don't let this sentence intimidate you. Everyone's form has been chosen for validation. This "validation" means that every college that you have applied to will want a copy of the student's and the parents' income tax returns. The validation usually stops there. However, FAAs may ask you to validate whatever they wish. If you have stated that other members of your family are also attending college, the FAAs may send you a form that must be filled out by an administrator at the college or colleges that the other family members are attending. Most colleges however, want nothing more than a copy of your tax forms.

College's own FAF forms

Many colleges require you to fill out their own financial aid form. Some of these forms are quite simple and don't ask for very much more information than you provide on a federal financial aid form. Other colleges have forms with questions that are not part of the congressional formula and are certain to invade your privacy. The reason for these questions is quite simple. The colleges realize that there are "loopholes" in the college financial aid system. Some of these voluntary answers will give the college insight into whether or not you are trying to use these loopholes. In many cases, these forms may intimidate parents enough that many families decide to not even apply for financial aid. Sample questions include:

- What you do for a living and how long you have worked for your present employer.
- The model and year of the car that you drive.
- The amount of money you have in your retirement fund.
- The cash value amount of your life insurance.
- The value of cash and assets in your younger children's names.

Some forms will even question if you have seen a financial planner in the last five years. Most colleges want nothing more than a copy of your W-2 and 1040 forms as verification of your financial aid form. Many parents therefore, are evasive when asked these personal questions. They feel that if an asset doesn't show up on your tax forms, it doesn't exist. After all, the total amount of your IRA doesn't show up on your tax form (just the amount taken out for the present year). The value of your life insurance doesn't show up, and certainly the amount of assets in your younger children's names doesn't show up. Because there is no way for colleges to check, lots of parents are tempted to leave these assets off of the *college's own* financial aid forms and feel justified in doing so because the colleges are asking them personal questions that are not part of the state and federal financial aid formulas.

Note: We are not telling you to lie or misrepresent your financial status. We just want you to be aware that you do not have to answer intrusive questions.

The following are examples of the college's own financial aid forms, from the least invasive to the most invasive, in my opinion.

Copies of all of the college's financial aid forms

Once you have looked at some of the colleges' own financial aid forms you will have some idea as to how intimidating some of these questions can be. I would like to point out the one question that seems to be on almost all of the forms—how much the parents plan to contribute towards the cost of education. Oh, it's usually worded as "parents' contribution from assets" and "parents' contribution from income." But no matter how they ask it, what they are asking is "how much money do you volunteer to pay?" Don't get yourself crazy thinking of how the administrators will psychologically interpret your answer. Just put in a very low number, one that is less than you would ever expect to pay. Colleges will automatically accept your answer if it is higher than the amount that they were going to ask you to pay. So don't put your foot in your mouth. That question is a trap.

FRESHMAN FINANCIAL AID APPLICATION
SEPTEMBER 1993 — MAY 1994

Confidential

OFFICE OF STUDENT AID AND FAMILY FINANCE, SARATOGA SPRINGS, NY 12866-1632, PHONE: 518-584-5000 EXT. 2144

TYPE OR PRINT IN INK ALL INFORMATION. ANSWER ALL QUESTIONS COMPLETELY.
Please refer to the enclosed instructions when completing this form and other required documents to ensure that you have a complete aid application. Return this form to: Skidmore College, Office of Student Aid and Family Finance, Saratoga Springs, NY 12866-1632.

Section A (to be completed by student) Please check the date for submission based on the appropriate admission plan.

____ December 1, 1992 .... Early Decision Round I

____ January 15, 1993 .... Early Decision Round II

____ February 1, 1993 .... Regular Decision Plan

PERSONAL INFORMATION:

Name of Candidate _____ Sex (optional) ____ Male ____ Female
          Last   First   Middle

Home Address _____
          Number and Street   City   County   State   Zip

Telephone ( )_____ ( )_____ Social Security No. _____
          Home   School   (optional)

Name of high school from which you will graduate _____

Are you a citizen of the United States? ____ Yes ____ No. If no, what is your country of citizenship? _____

Your alien registration number _____ Your visa status _____

Will you be a ____ resident or ____ commuter at Skidmore during 1993-94?

Do you have an interest in any assets in another person's name? ____ Yes ____ No   If yes,

Name of Person	Relationship	Description of Asset	Current Value

Will you have use of a motor vehicle during the 1993-94 academic year at Skidmore? ____ Yes ____ No

If yes, Make _____ Model _____ Year _____ Owner _____

Owner's Relationship to you _____ Purchase Price _____ Year of Purchase _____ Amount Owed _____

Section B (to be completed by student and parents) See instructions for "DEFINITION OF PARENTS SECTION" to understand how to complete the remainder of the form. Estimate how much money will be available from parents, student, and other sources to be contributed toward college costs (tuition, fees, room, and board) for the academic year 1993-94 from the following:

RESOURCES

Parents' Offer from Total Income .... $_____

Parents' Offer from Assets .... $_____

Parents' Offer from Loans .... $_____

Parent Tuition Benefit from Employer .... $_____

Expected Support from
Relatives and Friends (not parents) ..... $_____

Student Summer Earnings .... $_____

Other Sources .... $_____
(Please explain on next page. **Do not include aid you are applying for.**)

TOTAL .... $_____

STUDENT ASSETS

Bank Accounts, (Savings, NOW, CD) ..... $_____
current value

Stocks and Bonds, current market value ... $_____

Money Market or
Mutual Funds, current market value ... $_____

Trusts, (Clifford, Crown, Others) .... $_____
current market value

Single Premium Life Insurance, cash value .. $_____

Other Assets .... $_____
(Please explain on next page.)

Section D (to be completed by parents)

Marital status of parents with whom student resides:

_____ 1. *Never married

_____ 2. Married

_____ 3. *Separated

_____ 4. *Divorced, now remarried

_____ 5. *Divorced, now single

_____ 6. Widowed, now remarried

_____ 7. Widowed, now single

*NOTE: SPECIAL INSTRUCTIONS SECTION to complete application for this marital status.

* Is whereabouts of non-custodial parent (parent who does not reside in the same household as the student) known? ____ Yes ____ No

If yes, please provide the non-custodial parent's name, address, and telephone number. _____

_____

_____

Telephone: Father's Work (   ) _____ Occupation _____ Employer _____

Telephone: Mother's Work (   ) _____ Occupation _____ Employer _____

If parents expect to support other dependent children in college during the coming year (1993-94) in addition to the applicant, list each child's name, age, college, year in college, dollar amount of college expenses, and the amount you expect to contribute:

Name	Age	College	Year in College	$ College Expenses	$ Amount from Parents

Name	Age	College	Year in College	$ College Expenses	$ Amount from Parents

Did you have someone else (beside student and parents) prepare and/or assist in preparing the Financial Aid Form and/or student aid

application materials? _____ Yes _____ No.   If yes, list name and address of preparer and amount paid, if any, for preparation.

_____ $ _____

Did you ever engage the services of a financial planner? _____ Yes _____ No. If yes, what year was service rendered? _____

I/we expect to contribute $ _____ toward expenses of my/our child's 1993-94 academic year at Skidmore College.

I/we certify that the information on this application is true to the best of my/our knowledge at this time. I/we agree to complete and file the parents' section of the 1993-94 Financial Aid Form by the required Skidmore deadline and agree to forward a copy of my/our 1992 U.S. Federal Income Tax Return(s), with all pages, schedules, and W-2 forms or their equivalent (non-taxable income sources statement), as soon as they are available.

I/we agree to provide any additional information requested to enable the Office of Student Aid and Family Finance to evaluate this request for assistance and/or for continuing eligibility for any financial assistance program(s) administered by Skidmore. I/we authorize Skidmore College Student Aid staff to discuss my/our financial information with all of the colleges in which other members of my/our family are enrolled. In addition, I/we agree to send immediate notice of any significant change in information, family income, or assets, or college plans of other family members to Skidmore.

To assist in the determination of financial need I/we authorize Skidmore College Student Aid staff to discuss the information contained on this form and the Financial Aid Form with student. _____ Yes _____ No.

_____   _____

Signature of (check) _____ Father, _____ Stepfather, or _____ Legal Male Guardian   Date

_____   _____

Signature of (check) _____ Mother, _____ Stepmother, or _____ Legal Female Guardian   Date

Use the space below to explain any resource and student asset information.

_____

Please list other non-Skidmore grants/scholarships for which you are applying (source and amount). Put an asterisk (*) next to scholarship awards that are definite.

Grant/Scholarship	$ Amount
Grant/Scholarship	$ Amount

Please describe any unusual financial circumstances that may affect this request for assistance, including any 1993-94 expenses over which the student and family have no control.

_____
_____
_____

Section C (to be completed by parents) See instructions for "DEFINITION OF PARENTS SECTION."

Parents who: 1. own a home, or
               2. have total income of more than $15,000 in 1992
must complete Section C; otherwise, skip to Section D.

Monthly home mortgage (including principal, interest, and real estate taxes) or rental payment for home in which parents reside $ _____ .

If renting, landlord name and address and relationship, if any, to parents: _____
_____

If no rent or mortgage payment, please explain: _____

Do parents receive free housing as job benefit? _____ Yes _____ No

If yes, what is the average monthly rental payment for living units where parents live? $ _____

If parents own home: current tax assessment of its value .... $ _____	Was home refinanced? _____ Yes _____ No If yes, amount approved .... $ _____
Does this amount reflect a 100% assessed value? _____ Yes _____ No	Parents' Gross Income 1992 (estimate) .... $ _____
	Student's Gross Income 1992 (estimate) .. $ _____
Fire insurance coverage for home's replacement value (home only) is .. $ _____	Amount of life insurance coverage .... $ _____
	Cash value of single premium life insurance $ _____
Have parents had a home equity loan approved? _____ Yes _____ No	Current value of IRA/Keogh Plans .... $ _____
If yes, amount approved .... $ _____	Current value of other tax-deferred pensions, annuities, and savings plans (including but not limited to: SRA's, 401K, 403B, 408, 414H, 457, 501C, other _____) ;
Amount borrowed to date .... $ _____	
Date of equity loan approval .... _____	
Of the amount borrowed to date, what was the money used for? _____ _____	Circle your plan type(s) .... $ _____
	Value of assets over $1,000 held in the name of brothers/sisters in household ..
What is the principal balance on first mortgage? .... $ _____	Sibling Name _____ Value ... $ _____
	Sibling Name _____ Value ... $ _____

Do you participate in a tax-deferred pension plan? _____ Yes _____ No. If yes, are you required by your employer to contribute to the plan? _____ Yes _____ No. If yes, how much of the 1992 contribution was required by employer? $ _____

Do parents have an interest in any assets in another person's name? _____ Yes _____ No. If yes,

Name of Person	Relationship	Description of Asset	Current Value

Family Motor Vehicles (owned, leased, or business-owned; include automobiles and recreational vehicles):

Make/Model _____ Year _____ Purchase Price $ _____ Year of Purchase _____ Amount Owed $ _____

Make/Model _____ Year _____ Purchase Price $ _____ Year of Purchase _____ Amount Owed $ _____

Do parents own a boat? _____ Yes _____ No   Purchase Price $ _____ Year of Purchase _____ Amount Owed $ _____

Do either of the parents own a business or farm or is either self-employed? _____ Yes _____ No

If yes, please forward a copy or copies of the 1991 or the most recent Federal Tax Schedule C, Schedule F, corporation, and/or partnership return to the Office of Student Aid and Family Finance.

Section E (to be completed by student)

SKIDMORE COLLEGE STATEMENT OF UNDERSTANDING

All students applying for any type of student aid must read and sign the following:

I certify that the information on this application is true to the best of my knowledge at this time. I agree to file an accurate 1993-94 Financial Aid Form by the required Skidmore deadline and will provide a copy of my own 1992 U.S. Federal Tax Return, with all pages, schedules, and W-2 forms or their equivalent (non-taxable income sources statement), as soon as they are available.

I understand the responsibilities incurred by this application (as outlined in the instructions enclosed with this application) and agree to provide additional information that may be necessary for the evaluation of my application and/or for continuing my eligibility for any financial assistance program(s) administered by Skidmqre. In addition, I agree to send immediate notice of any change in information to Skidmore, including the receipt of other scholarships or grants not previously reported.

I authorize Skidmore Student Aid staff to discuss my application with other colleges, donors, agencies, or organizations that may also be considering me for aid. To assist in determining financial need, I authorize the Student Aid staff to discuss the information contained in my application materials and the Financial Aid Form with my parents.

Student's Signature _____ Date _____

STUDENT STATEMENT OF EDUCATIONAL PURPOSE

I will use all Title IV money received — Pell, SEOG, Perkins Loan (formerly NDSL), CWSP, Stafford Student Loan (formerly GSL), PLUS and SLS — only for expenses related to my study at Skidmore College. I understand that I am responsible for repaying any funds I receive that cannot reasonably be attributed to meeting my educational expenses at Skidmore College.

I certify that I do not owe a refund on any grant, am not in default on any loan, and have not borrowed in excess of the loan limits under Title IV programs, at any institution. I am also aware that in order to continue to receive assistance from any Title IV programs, I must maintain satisfactory progress in the course of study I am pursuing according to the standards and practices of Skidmore College.

STUDENT STATEMENT OF REGISTRATION STATUS

_____ I certify that I am registered with the Selective Service.

_____ I certify that I am not required to be registered with the Selective Service, because:

    _____ I am female.

    _____ I am in the armed services on active duty.
    (Note: Does not apply to members of the Reserves and National Guard who are not on active duty.)

    _____ I have not reached my 18th birthday.

    _____ I was born before 1960.

    _____ I am a citizen of the Federated States of Micronesia, the Marshall Islands,
    or a permanent resident of the Trust Territory of the Pacific Islands (Palau).

STUDENT ANTI-DRUG ABUSE ACT CERTIFICATION

_____ I certify that, as a condition of my Pell Grant, I will not engage in the unlawful manufacture, distribution, dispensation, possession, or use of a controlled substance during the period covered by my Pell Grant.

I declare under penalty of perjury that the foregoing is true and correct.

Student's Signature _____ Date _____

(These statements cover the period of July 1, 1993 to June 30, 1994.)

OPTIONAL

_____ I grant permission and request that routine copies of my student aid and amended awards be sent (first-class U.S. mail) to the address of my parent of record (address within Skidmore College data system) when I am on campus during the academic year.

Student's Signature _____ Date _____

Mail to: Carnegie Mellon Financial Aid Office, 5000 Forbes Ave., Pittsburgh, PA 15213-3890. Fax to: (412) 268-7837.
If you have questions, call the financial aid staff at (412) 268-2068.
COMPLETE BOTH SIDES. Please attach additional information only in answer to questions on form.

Parental Financial Data

- Parents' current marital status (check one) .... married   widowed   divorced/separated
  (If separated or divorced, Carnegie Mellon will normally expect a contribution from the non-custodial parent unless documentation can be provided which reflects that such an expectation is unreasonable.)

- Age of the older parent with whom you reside .... _____

- Number of 1992 taxable dependents .... _____
  (Include parents as well as children; if you do not file a tax return, answer this question as if you did file.)

- Number of students in college for the upcoming 1993-94 academic year .... _____
  Please list below only dependent, undergraduate children expected to enroll full time in college for the 1993-94 academic year.
  Do not include parents. You *must* include information for each student in order for the aid office to process your application.

Student's name(s)	Age	Name of undergraduate college to be attended in 1993-94	Year in school in 1993-94 academic year

- Father's estimated 1992 wages, tips and other compensation... $_____

- Mother's estimated 1992 wages, tips and other compensation... $_____

- All other estimated 1992 parental taxable income .... $_____
  (Including, but not limited to rents, interests, pensions, alimony, etc.)

- Child support received in 1992 .... $_____

- Number of individuals for whom child support is received .... _____

- All other estimated 1992 parental non-taxable income .... $_____
  (Include interest from non-taxable bonds, parent's Social Security benefits, tax-deferred compensation, etc. Include the student's 1992 Social Security benefits. *Any losses and/or adjustments to income should not be included*.)

- Will parents file a federal income tax return for 1992?   Yes   No   If yes, what type of return?   1040   1040A   1040EZ

- If parents will file a 1040, will they itemize deductions on Schedule A?   Yes   No
  If yes, what will be the total deductions itemized in 1992? .... $_____

- Estimate of 1992 federal taxes to be paid (not withheld) .... $_____

- 1992 unreimbursed elementary and secondary tuition expenses (*exclude the applicant*) .... $_____
  (Also, exclude any expenses related to post-secondary educational expenses.)

- Number of students for whom this expense was incurred (do not include students enrolled in college) .... _____

- Parents' current cash, savings, checking accounts, etc... $_____

	Year Purchased	Purchase Price	Current Market Value	Current Outstanding Mortgage
Home				
Other real estate				
Other real estate				

(If there are more than two other pieces of real estate, please attach the above information for each property on a separate piece of paper.)

- Net market value of investments (Include stocks, bonds, etc. *Do not* include business, farm or retirement funds.) .... $_____

- Net market value of business or farm .... $_____
  (Total market value of land, buildings, etc., minus unpaid principal and related debts. *Do not* include net value of home. If your family is part owner of a business or farm, list only parents' share of the net worth.)

- Estimate of parents' ability to contribute to a Carnegie Mellon education .... $_____

Note: The data provided will result in an estimate of expected family contribution to meet college costs EXCEPT IN SOME CASES OF DIVORCE/SEPARATION AND/OR SELF-EMPLOYMENT. In such cases the financial aid staff may need additional details from your tax return.

Please Read and Sign

_____   _____   _____
Student's Signature   Parent's Signature   Date

Forms received after December 1, 1992 will not be processed.

Office of Admission
Carnegie Mellon University
5000 Forbes Avenue
Pittsburgh, PA 15213-3890

Phone: (412) 268-2082
Fax: (412) 268-7838

Carnegie Mellon News • Financial Aid

September 1992 / Vol. 19 / No. 2 / B-045 / 75M
Name of Publication: Carnegie Mellon University/Subtitle:
Envision, Financial Aid News, Parents News, Student News/
Frequency of Issue: Published four times a year. Once in
July and December. Twice in September/ Publisher's
Address: Carnegie Mellon University, University Publications
Department, Publications and Printing Building, Pittsburgh,
Pennsylvania 15213-3890/Second class postage paid in
Pittsburgh, Pennsylvania/USPS 442-370

This newsletter is printed on recycled paper.

For an estimate of your financial aid package, complete both sides of this form and return it to us. We must receive your information no later than December 1, 1992, to give you an estimate before you apply for admission.

Questions? Call Financial Aid at (412) 268-2068.

Students who intend to apply for admission through early decision should not complete this form.

1993-94 Financial Aid Early Estimate—Part Two

**Mail to: Carnegie Mellon Financial Aid Office, 5000 Forbes Ave., Pittsburgh, PA 15213-3890 Fax to: (412) 268-7837
If you have questions, call the Financial Aid staff at (412) 268-2068.
COMPLETE BOTH SIDES.**

Student Data Please provide as complete information as possible for the upcoming academic year.

Student's social security number ☐☐☐ ☐☐ ☐☐☐☐

Student's name _____

Student's complete mailing address _____
(Please include your city, state and zip)

If the Carnegie Mellon financial aid staff has questions, they can reach us during business hours at ☐☐☐ - ☐☐☐ - ☐☐☐☐

Rank in class _____ Class size_____   Are you a U.S. citizen? ☐ Yes ☐ No
(If you believe you are an eligible non-citizen, please include copies of
SAT verbal _____ SAT math_____   documentation defining your status and check "yes.")

Intended field of study_____   Student's savings and net assets............................. $_____
Are any of these assets comprised of parent savings?
If so, how much?... $_____

ADDITIONAL TERMS OF THE PROMISSORY NOTE FOR A STUDENT LOAN GUARANTEED BY NYSHESC

II. DATE NOTE COMES DUE. I will repay this loan: 1) in periodic installments during a repayment period that will by law begin no later than the end of my grace period on a Stafford Loan or from date of disbursement on an SLS loan. SLS loans will not be eligible for a grace period; or 2) in full immediately if I fail to enroll and attend the school which certified my application for the academic period intended; 3) immediately in full, if this loan was made or guaranteed in error or in reliance upon a false statement. My grace period on a Stafford Loan is that period of time which begins when either I leave school or stop carrying at an eligible school approved by the United States Department of Education at least one-half the normal full-time academic work load required by the school. The Notice of Loan Guarantee and Disclosure Statement will identify the length of my grace period if any. During the grace period I may request that the grace period be shortened and the repayment period begin earlier.

III. INTEREST. (1) I agree to pay an amount equivalent to simple interest (as specified in (4)) on the unpaid principal balance from the date of disbursement until the entire principal sum and accrued interest are paid in full. (2) However, the U.S. Secretary ("Secretary") will pay the interest that accrues on the Stafford loan prior to repayment status and during any deferment if it is determined that I qualify to have such payments made on my behalf under the regulations governing the Stafford Loan Program. In the event that the interest on this loan is payable by the Secretary, neither the lender nor other holder of the Note may attempt to collect this interest from me. I may, however, choose to pay this interest myself. (3) Once the repayment status begins, I will be responsible for payment of all interest that accrues on this loan, except that if the interest accruing on this loan prior to the repayment period was payable by the Secretary, the Secretary will pay the interest that accrues during any period described under DEFERMENT in this Promissory Note. (4) I understand that this application may be used for both the Stafford Loan and Supplemental Loans for Students ("SLS") programs, that the interest terms for such loans are different and are determined according to the following rules established by law. If I have an outstanding Stafford loan(s) on the date I sign this Note, the applicable interest rate will be the same as the applicable interest rate on the outstanding Stafford loan(s). (b) If I have no outstanding Stafford loan(s) but I do have an outstanding balance on any PLUS or SLS loan(s) made for enrollment periods beginning before July 1, 1988, or on any Consolidation loan(s) which repaid loans made for enrollment period(s) beginning before that date, the applicable interest rate on this loan will be 8%. (c) If I have no outstanding balance on any Stafford, PLUS or SLS loan(s) made for enrollment period(s) beginning before July 1, 1988, or on any Consolidation loan(s) which repaid loans made for enrollment period(s) beginning before that date, the applicable interest rate on this loan will be 8% until the end of the fourth year of my repayment status and will be 10% beginning with the fifth year of my repayment status. (5) The applicable interest rate (a) until the end of the fourth year of my repayment status, and (b) beginning with the fifth year of my repayment status, will be identified on the (Notice of Disclosure). (6) I may also receive rebates of interest, if required by the Higher Education Act of 1965, as amended, when the applicable interest rate is 10%. The interest rate on the SLS loan will vary annually on July 1, but, in no event will the rate exceed 12%. At the option of the lender either the amount of the monthly payment or the length of the repayment period will be adjusted in order to reflect changes in the interest rate in subsequent years. (7) The lender or other holder of this note may add accrued interest to the unpaid principal balance (capitalization) of this loan in accordance with regulations/policies of the New York State Higher Education Services Corporation.

IV. ORIGINATION AND INSURANCE FEES. I will pay you an origination fee on a Stafford Loan as authorized by federal law not to exceed the amount identified on the Notice of Loan Guarantee and Disclosure Statement. I will pay to the lender an amount equal to the fee that the lender is required to pay to the guarantee agency to obtain insurance coverage on this loan. If the lender does not withhold this premium from the principal amount of the loan and I have not already paid the premium, I will pay the premium when the lender bills me separately for it. The origination fee and the insurance premium may both be deducted from the proceeds of my loan. In the event of a multiple disbursement the insurance premium will be deducted proportionately.

V. DEFAULT. Default occurs when I fail to make an installment payment when due, or to meet other terms of the Application and Promissory Note, or under circumstances where NYSHESC finds it reasonable to conclude that I no longer intend to honor the obligation to repay, provided that my failure persists for (a) 180 days if I repay in monthly installments, or (b) 240 days if I am obligated to repay in installments due less frequently. If I default, my lender will ask NYSHESC to purchase my loan, at which time I will owe the entire balance of the loan to NYSHESC directly, and I will be ineligible to receive assistance from any of the following Federal programs: Pell Grant, Supplemental Educational Opportunity Grant, College Work-Study, State Student Incentive Grant, Byrd Scholarship, Perkins Loan (formerly called National Direct Student Loan), Stafford Loans, Supplemental Student Loans (SLS), PLUS Loans, Income Contingent Loans or Consolidation Loans. NYSHESC may disclose to schools I have attended or am currently attending the information about the default. In the event that bankruptcy proceedings are commenced by or against me, I specifically agree to notify NYSHESC of such occurrence in writing within twenty (20) days of the filing of a petition.

VI. DEFAULT AND LATE CHARGES. I agree to pay, in the event of default, reasonable attorney's fees plus costs and other charges necessary to collect any amount not paid when due. If I fail to make all or part of a scheduled monthly payment within 10 days of its due date the lender may assess a late charge not to exceed six cents for each dollar of each late installment.

VII. ADDITIONAL AGREEMENTS. 1) The proceeds of this loan will be used only for my education expenses at the school indicated in Part B of my application. 2) Any notice required to be given to me will be effective when mailed by first class mail to the latest address you have for me. 3) Your failure to enforce or insist that I comply with any term of this Note is not a waiver of your rights. No provision of this Note can be waived or modified except in writing. 4) If NYSHESC is required under its guarantee to repay my loan(s) because I have defaulted, NYSHESC will have all rights of the original lender to recover on this Note or under the guarantee; 5) I understand that I must repay this Note even though I may be under 18 years of age; 6) If I am unable to make the scheduled payments for reason of hardship, I may at the discretion of the lender be eligible for forbearance on the repayment of my loan(s) as provided for in the NYSHESC regulations; 7) If I go into default on this loan I agree to be sued in Albany County, New York. 8) In this Note the words, I, me, and my mean the borrower identified in item 7 of Part A of the Application. You, your and yours mean the lender and any other owner of the Note.

VIII. DEFERMENT. You will let me pay interest only (if such interest is not paid by the United States Government) and let me defer making principal payments on this Note as provided below if my repayment period has begun, I am not in default, and I can provide you with written evidence that I qualify for the deferment: 1) While I am enrolled a) at a participating school in full-time study as determined by that school, however, to obtain a deferment to attend a school not located in the United States, I must be a citizen or national of the United States, or b) in an eligible graduate fellowship program, or c) in a rehabilitation training program for disabled individuals, or d) as a full-time student at an institution of higher education or vocational school which is operated by an agency of the United States Government. 2) For periods not exceeding 3 years for each of the following while I am a) on active duty in the Armed Forces of the United States or serving as an officer in the Commissioned Corps of the United States Public Health Service, or b) serving as a Peace Corps volunteer, or c) serving as a full-time volunteer under Title I of the Domestic Volunteer Service Act of 1973 (e.g. VISTA), or d) providing service as a full-time volunteer for an organization exempt from Federal Income Tax under Section 501(c)(3) of the Internal Revenue Code of 1954, which the Secretary of Education has determined is comparable to service performed in the Peace Corps or ACTION program, e) temporarily totally disabled, as established by affidavit of a qualified physician, or unable to work because I am providing care required by a spouse or another dependent who is temporarily totally disabled as established by affidavit of a qualified physician. 3) For a period not exceeding 2 years while I am serving an internship that is needed to gain professional recognition required to begin professional practice or service, or periods not exceeding 2 years during which I am serving in an internship or residency program leading to a degree or certificate awarded by an institution of higher education, a hospital, or a health care facility that offers postgraduate training. (The cumulative time period for these deferments is 2 years) 4) For a maximum aggregate of twenty four months while I am conscientiously seeking but unable to find full-time employment in the United States; 5) For a period not in excess of six months for parental leave. If I am new borrower for a period of enrollment beginning on or after July 1, 1987, or a loan is disbursed on or after July 1, 1987, the following deferments are also available: 1) While I am enrolled at a participating school in at least half-time study as determined by that school if I obtain a loan under Part B of Title IV of the Higher Education Act during such period of enrollment; 2) for periods not exceeding three years during which I am (a) an active duty member of the National Oceanic and Atmospheric Administration Corps (the 3 year limit includes any deferment time taken for Military and or Public Health Service), or (b) during which I am engaged as a full-time teacher in a public or nonprofit private elementary or secondary school in a teacher shortage area established by the United States Secretary of Education. 3) For a period not in excess of twelve months for mothers of pre-school age children entering or re-entering the work force and who are compensated at a rate not in excess of $1.00 more than the minimum wage prescribed by Section 6 of the Fair Labor Standards Act of 1938.

IX. REPAYMENT. I will repay the total amount of this Promissory Note with interest in periodic installments unless the whole loan becomes due and payable as described in Paragraph II, "Date Note Comes Due" or Paragraph V, "Default." I agree to immediately notify in writing the lender or NYSHESC when I leave school, drop to less than half-time, or fail to enroll for the academic period in the school for which the loan was made. I understand you will send to me a Repayment Schedule which shows the particular repayment terms that will become part of this Promissory Note. The Repayment Schedule may include all loans I have received from you under the NYSHESC Stafford Loan or SLS Program. I understand that this is not a demand instrument and my obligation to begin timely repayment of principal and interest will not be forgiven for any reason, including lender or NYSHESC error except upon consent of NYSHESC.

The Repayment Schedule will require me to make monthly payments for a period of not less than 5 nor more than 10 years after this Note becomes due not counting periods for which I am granted any authorized deferment outlined in Deferment Paragraph VIII, or forbearance. At my option I may agree to a repayment period that is shorter than 5 years, however, I may at a later time have the repayment period extended so that the total repayment period is not less than 5 years. On loans disbursed on or after October 1, 1981 the total payments for any year of the repayment period on all loans received under Title IV, Part B of the Higher Education Act of 1965 as amended shall not be less than $600 per year including payments by my spouse on any loan under such loan programs (or the balance of all such loans plus accrued interest if less than $600) even though this may result in a repayment period shorter than 5 years.

X. PREPAYMENT. I may, at my option and without penalty, prepay all or any part of the principal or accrued interest of this loan at any time. If I do so, I will be entitled to a rebate of any unearned interest that I have paid.

XI. CREDIT BUREAU NOTIFICATION. Pursuant to law, you will report the following information concerning this loan to credit reporting agencies: 1) the total amount of loans made to me under this part and the remaining balance of the loans; 2) information concerning the date and amount of any default and subsequent collection activity including the status of any defaulted loan upon which payments have been made. If I default on this loan, the lender, holder or NYSHESC will also report the default to one or more credit bureau organizations. This may significantly and adversely affect my ability to obtain other credit. My lender, holder or NYSHESC must notify me at least 30 days in advance that information about the default will be disclosed to credit bureau organizations, unless I enter into repayment on the loan within the 30 days; 3) the date of cancellation of the loan for any reason established by law for such cancellation including death, permanent and total disability, and bankruptcy. The lender must provide a timely response to a request from any credit bureau organization regarding objections I might raise with that organization about the accuracy and completion of information reported about me.

BORROWER CERTIFICATION.

I declare under penalty of law that the information contained in Part A of this application is true, complete and correct to the best of my knowledge and belief and is made in good faith. I hereby authorize the school to pay to the lender any refund which may be due me up to the amount of this loan. I further authorize any school that I may attend to release to the lending institution, subsequent holder, NYSHESC, U.S. Department of Education, or their agents any requested information pertinent to this loan (e.g. employment, enrollment status, current address). I agree that the proceeds of any loan made as a result of this application will be used for educational expenses for the loan period covered by this application at the school named in Part B. I understand that I must immediately repay any refunds that I receive which cannot reasonably be attributed to meeting my educational expenses related to attendance at that school for the loan period stated in Item 24 of this application or which are in excess of the maximum annual or aggregate loan amounts established by Part B of Title IV of the Higher Education Act of 1965, as amended. I further certify that I do not owe a refund on a Pell Grant, Supplemental Grant or State Student Incentive Grant or Byrd Scholarship and I am not now in default on a Perkins Loan (National Direct Student Loan) or a Stafford Loan, or a Federally Insured Student Loan or a PLUS or SLS loan, Income Contingent Loan or Consolidation Loan. I further authorize my lending institution to make any check for the proceeds of my loan, jointly payable to me and the school named in Part B of this application, unless I am attending a foreign school, in which case the check will be made payable only to me. I have read and understand the "Statement of Borrower's Rights and Responsibilities" supplied with this application.

I understand that I will receive a Notice of Loan Guarantee and Disclosure Statement that identifies my loan amount, the fee rates and amounts, due dates, and grace period.

NOTICE TO STUDENT: BY YOUR SIGNATURE ON THE OTHER SIDE OF THIS APPLICATION AND PROMISSORY NOTE YOU ARE AGREEING TO THE ABOVE TERMS AND CERTIFICATIONS.

6. LOANS

Throughout this book, I have directed myself to the parents of the students. They are the ones paying the bills. However, since a **Stafford Loan** can only be taken out by students, and it is the students' sole responsibility to repay this loan, I would like for parents to make sure their children read this particular segment. I know that in *many* cases, the students' name on the loan form is only a formality and many parents will pay back these loans for their children. I also know that in many cases it is the parents who walk into the bank and ask for a Stafford Loan form, fill it out, and then ask their children to sign it. However, because it is the students who must undertake the legal responsibility for the loan, it is the students who should read this segment of the chapter so that they know what they and their parents are getting into. Students and parents should consider:

1. How much money they may be eligible to borrow, and
2. Just what their obligations, responsibilities, and rights are in regard to paying back this money.

The Higher Education Act of 1992 is now a reality. Congress' answer to the rise in college education costs that has taken place over the last five years is to allow you to borrow more money. All students, regardless of financial need, will be able to get student loans in their own names. This new loan program is called the **Federal Unsubsidized Stafford Loan**. It has the same interest rate and borrowing limits as the current Stafford Loan. However, there is a big difference between the two programs.

When you borrow under the new unsubsidized loan program, you are responsible to pay the interest that accrues on the loan while you are in school. You can pay the interest monthly or you can have the interest added to the total of the loan. This is called capitalization. Under the regular Stafford Loan program, there is no interest on the loans for as long as you are in school. Interest doesn't start until six months after you leave school. So, being eligible for the regular Stafford Loan can save you thousands of dollars in interest costs.

EXAMPLE. A student borrowing $2,000 per year for four consecutive years owes approximately $8,000 at the end of that four-year period under the regular Stafford program.

The same student who borrows $2,000 per year for four years under the unsubsidized Stafford program and who capitalizes the interest, owes about $10,000 after the same four-year period.

What is the Stafford Loan?

The Stafford Loan is certainly the most popular education loan. Stafford Loans are low-interest loans made to students attending college at least *half-time*. Loans are by a lender such as a bank, credit union, or savings and loan association. Sometimes a school acts as a lender. These loans are insured by the **guarantee agency** in each state and reinsured by the federal government. You must repay this loan.

What is the interest rate?

Not only is this a great loan with an interest rate that you could never match in a business or personal loan situation, but it is interest free until after you graduate or leave school. The interest rate on the Stafford Loan is variable and is tied to the **U.S. Treasury bill rate**. The rate is 3.1% over the Treasury bill rate with a maximum interest rate of 9%.

How much can I borrow?

Before assuming that you will want to borrow the maximum amount allowed, please remember that a Stafford Loan must be paid back. Your minimum monthly payment will be based on how much you owe. So before you borrow, know what your minimum payments are going to be, just as you would on any installment purchase.

For both types of Stafford Loans, the limits are as follows:

First year undergraduates	$2,625
Second year undergraduates	3,500

Third year undergraduates	5,500
Fourth year undergraduates	5,500
Graduate loan per year	8,500

The aggregate loan limit for undergraduates is $23,000.

The aggregate loan limit for graduate studies is $65,000, including undergraduate education.

The interest rate charged will be the U.S. Treasury bill rate plus 3.1% capped at 9%.

The loans are strictly the student's responsibility. Parents *do not* underwrite these loans.

Note: You can't borrow more than the cost of education at your school, minus your family contribution and any other financial aid you receive.

How do I apply?

You won't have to look hard to find a Stafford Loan application. Just walk into your neighborhood bank and ask for one. Almost all the banks carry them. You can also get an application from a lender, a school, or your state guarantee agency. When you are finished, the school you plan to attend must complete its part. It will certify your enrollment, your cost of education, your academic standing, any other financial aid you'll receive, and your financial need. It will be mailed back to you.

You must apply for a Pell Grant before you can be eligible for a Stafford Loan. Even if you are denied a Pell Grant, you can still receive a Stafford Loan. If you're eligible, the amount of your Pell Grant will be considered in determining your financial aid package so that you won't be over-awarded.

You or the school will submit the completed application to the lender you have chosen. If the lender agrees to make the loan and gets the approval of the guarantee agency, the lender will send the loan amount to your school in at least two payments.

The school may or may not approve your loan application, and, even if it does, it may not be for the amount you have requested. The decision is the school's and cannot be appealed.

When should I apply?

Once you have received an award letter verifying that you are eligible for a Stafford Loan, you should walk to your favorite bank and pick up an application.

Application and Promissory Note for a Stafford Loan

WARNING: Any person who knowingly makes a false statement or misrepresentation on this form is subject to penalties which may include fines or imprisonment under the United States Criminal Code and 20 USC 1097.

SECTION I — TO BE COMPLETED BY THE STUDENT — READ THE INSTRUCTIONS — TYPE OR PRINT IN INK

1 Social Security Number

2 Last Name, First, Middle Initial, Permanent Home Address

3 Birthdate

4 Driver's License

State   Number

5 Area Code/Telephone Number

6 U.S. Citizenship Status (Check one) ☐ 1 Citizen ☐ 2 Eligible Non-Citizen   **Alien ID Number**

7 References – You must provide 3 separate adult references with different addresses. If your Lender requires a cosigner, make the cosigner your first reference. (Carefully read instructions.)

Name	Name	Name
Street Address	Street Address	Street Address
City, State, Zip	City, State, Zip	City, State, Zip
Telephone ( )	Telephone ( )	Telephone ( )
Employer	Employer	Employer

8 Intended Enrollment Status (Check one) ☐ 1 Full-time ☐ 2 At least half-time

9 Major Course of Study

10 Requested Loan Amount .00

11 Loan Period For this Loan. Mo. Yr. From   To   Mo. Yr.

12 Have you ever defaulted on an education loan? (Check one) If yes, carefully read instructions and attach required documentation. ☐ Yes ☐ No

13 Do you have any unpaid Stafford Loans or a Consolidation Loan with a Stafford portion? (Check one) If yes, carefully read instructions, complete 13A through 13E. If no, complete 13A through 13E with zeroes. ☐ Yes ☐ No

13A Total unpaid balance of your **most recent** Stafford Loan. .00

13B Use chart provided in instructions.

13C Grade level of your **most recent** Stafford Loan.

13D Beginning and ending dates of your **most recent** Stafford Loan. Mo. Yr. From   To   Mo. Yr

13E Total unpaid balance of all your Stafford Loans or any portion of your Stafford Loans included in a Consolidation Loan. .00

14 Do you have any outstanding Stafford, PLUS or SLS Loans made for enrollment periods beginning before July 1, 1988 or a Consolidation Loan which repaid loans for enrollment periods beginning before such date? ☐ Yes ☐ No

15 Name and Address of Previous Lender, if any.

Promissory Note for a Stafford Loan

I. Promise To Pay. I, the undersigned Borrower, promise to pay you or your order when this Note becomes due a sum certain equal to the loan amount I have requested in Section I, Item 10 of this Application or any lesser amount which will be disclosed to me in the Notice of Loan Guarantee and Disclosure Statement or the amount advanced to me, plus interest and any other charges which may become due as provided in Paragraph VI. My signature certifies I have read, understand and agree to the conditions and authorizations stated in the "Borrower Certification" printed on the reverse side and the legally required information highlighted in the Application Booklet.

Notice to Student: Terms of the Promissory Note continue on the reverse side. Retain Copy D for your records.

I understand this is a Promissory Note. I will not sign this Promissory Note before reading it, including the writing on the reverse side, even if otherwise advised. As a Borrower, I am entitled to an exact copy of this Promissory Note, the Notice of Loan Guarantee and Disclosure Statement and any agreement I sign. By signing this Promissory Note I, the Borrower, acknowledge I have received an exact copy of this Note.

20A X _____ Signature of Student Borrower   Date

SECTION II — TO BE COMPLETED BY THE SCHOOL

21 Name and Address of School

22 School Code

23 Area Code/Telephone Number

24 Grade Level Code

25 Anticipated Completion Date Mo. Yr.

26 Enrollment Period Covered by Loan Mo. Day Yr. Mo. Day Yr.

27 Family Adjusted Gross Income .00

28 Estimated Cost of Attendance for Loan Period .00

29 Estimated Financial Aid for Loan Period .00

30 Expected Family Contribution .00

31 Difference (28 minus the sum of 29 and 30) .00

32 Reduced Stafford Eligibility .00

33 Recommended Disbursement Date(s) **must** be completed Mo. Day Yr. Mo. Day Yr. Mo. Day Yr.

34 I have read and understand the terms of the SCHOOL CERTIFICATION printed on the back of the Application. Signature of Financial Aid Officer   Type or Print Name and Title   Date

SECTION III — TO BE COMPLETED BY THE LENDER

36 Name, City and State of Lending Institution

37 Lender Code

38 Area Code/Telephone Number

39 Loan Amount Approved .00

40 Interest Rate %

41 Anticipated Disbursement Date(s) Mo. Day Yr. Mo. Day Yr. Mo. Day Yr.

42 Fee

43 Authorized Lending Officer   Type or Print Name and Title   Date

44 For Lender Use Only

USA Funds Form 115C (2/91) B-6

It's as simple as that. Just about every lending institution in America participates in this loan program. It's what they call "money in the bank."

How do I qualify?

You must be attending school at least half-time.

To determine if you're eligible, the Department of Education uses a standard formula, passed into law by Congress, to evaluate the information you report on your student aid application.

Is there a charge for a Stafford Loan?

Yes. This is one of those facts that is kept very low-key. Not only is there a fee, but the total fees amount to 8% of the loan. That's right, the student who gets the maximum Stafford Loan each year will not only owe $23,000 upon graduation, but will also have paid $1,840 in fees for the privilege of owing it. There's an "origination fee" of 5% which will be deducted proportionately from each loan disbursement made to you. The money is passed on to the federal government to help reduce the government's cost of subsidizing these low-interest loans.

Your lender may also charge you an insurance premium of up to 3% of the loan principal. This premium must be deducted proportionately from each disbursement.

How will I be paid?

You won't be. Uncle Sam has gotten a little smarter over the years, and now sends the money directly to the college. This way, the government is guaranteed that all of the funds put aside for this program are used solely for education.

Your college account is credited in two payments, coinciding with the beginning of the academic terms, unless you are attending a foreign school, when one payment is made.

No payment may exceed one-half of the loan amount. If you're a first-year undergraduate student who is also a first-time Stafford Loan borrower, you can't receive your first payment until 30 days after the first day of your program of study begins. A 30-day wait also applies to *all* first-time Stafford Loan borrowers attending schools with a **default** rate of over 30%. (See your financial aid administrator for more information.)

When do I pay back this loan?

Three events trigger the requirement to repay the loans: they are graduation, dropping below half-time enrollment, or leaving school. You have a six-month grace period. Since this grace period sometimes varies in length with the terms of your promissory note, it is wise to check it out first. You may be allowed up to 10 years to repay.

The form on p. 78 is a copy of a Stafford Loan form.

The student fills in numbers 1 through 18 and signs the form. The form is then sent to the college financial aid office and the school will do the rest.

Perkins Loan

What is a Perkins Loan?

This program used to be called "National Direct Student Loans," but was renamed after the late congressman Carl D. Perkins of Kentucky, who was chairman of the House Education and Labor Committee.

The **Perkins Loan**, like the Stafford Loan, is the sole responsibility of the student. It is the best loan there is, because like the Stafford Loan (subsidized version only) there is no interest while the student is attending college, and the interest rate is only 5%; however, the Perkins Loan is available only to first-time college undergraduates, and usually only those who have received a Pell Grant.

Your school is the lender. You must repay this loan.

How much can I receive?

For federal Perkins Loans, the limits are as follows:
Undergraduate $3,000 per year limit.
Graduate $5,000 per year limit.

Aggregate loan limits

Undergraduate $15,000 aggregate loan limit.
Graduate and professional student $40,000 limit.

How will I be paid?

After you sign a **promissory note** agreeing to repay the loan, your school will either pay you directly or credit your account. You'll receive the loan in at least two payments during the academic year. (There's one exception: If the total

Perkins Loan you receive is $500 or less, the school may choose to pay you just once during the academic year.)

When do I pay back this loan?

Repayment terms are identical with the Stafford Loan.

How much will I have to pay each month?

The amount you pay each month is a simple function of how much you have borrowed, for how long, and at what interest rate. However, there are circumstances, such as ill-health and unemployment, which may influence the school to lower its monthly demands and to give you more time to pay off the full loan.

The following chart shows typical monthly payments and total interest charges for three different 5% loans over a 10-year period.

Total Loan Amount	Number of Payments	Monthly Payment	Total Interest Charges	Total Repayment
4,500	120	47.74	1,227.60	5,727.60
9,000	120	95.46	2,455.20	11,455.2
18,000	120	190.92	4,910.40	22,910.40

Source: Federal Student Guide, Department of Education.

Note: If you skip a payment, if it's late, or if you make less than a full payment, you'll have to pay a late charge plus any collection costs. Late charges will continue until your payments are current.

Is it ever possible to defer (postpone) repayment of a Perkins Loan?

Yes, under certain conditions— as long as your loan is not in default. Deferments are not automatic, however. You have to apply for one through your school, using a deferment request form obtained from your school. You must file your deferment request on time, or you will pay a late charge.

Note: Even though you may have *applied* for a deferment, you must *continue to make payments* until your deferment is processed. If you don't, you may end up in *default.* You should keep a copy of your deferment request form, and you should document all contacts with your school.

For more detail on deferments, contact your financial aid administrator.

PARENT LOAN APPLICATION

PL 100(4/89)

WARNING: Any person who knowingly makes a false statement or misrepresentation on this form is subject to penalties which include fines or imprisonment under the U.S. Criminal Code and USC 1097.

Higher Education Services Corporation

PART 1A—TO BE COMPLETED BY BORROWER   IMPORTANT—READ THE INSTRUCTIONS CAREFULLY

PART 1A

1. SOCIAL SECURITY NUMBER

2. NAME

Last   First   MI

3. BIRTHDATE

Month   Day   Year

4. PERMANENT HOME ADDRESS

(include Box or Apt. Number)

5. AREA CODE/PHONE NUMBER

City, Town or Village (Abbreviate if necessary)   State   Zip Code

6. Have you been a legal resident of NYS for 12 months immediately prior to the beginning of the academic period of this loan?
1 ☐ YES   2 ☐ NO

7. Do you currently have a student loan guaranteed by New York State? (NYHEAC or NYSHESC) (Check One)
1 ☐ YES   2 ☐ NO

8. REQUESTED LOAN AMOUNT
● $ _____

9. U.S. Citizenship Status
● 1 ☐ Citizen   2 ☐ Eligible Non-citizen
Alien Registration Number

10. Have you received a PLUS, Stafford (GSL), SLS (ALAS), FISL or Consolidation Loan for a period of enrollment that began, or was disbursed, on or after July 1, 1987 from any State (Include New York State) or Agency? (See Instructions Item 10)   1 ☐ YES   2 ☐ NO

11. Do you wish to defer principal payments while the student, for whom you borrow this loan, is attending school on a **full time** basis?   1 ☐ YES   2 ☐ NO

12. LENDER NAME & ADDRESS _____

BORROWER

13. REFERENCES—(REFERENCES MUST RESIDE IN THE UNITED STATES) SEE INSTRUCTIONS

Nearest Living Adult Relative   Nearest Living Adult Relative Not Residing at Address indicated in item 13A.

Name (A) _____   Name (B) _____

Address _____   City _____   Address _____   City _____

State _____   Zip _____   Telephone No. _____   State _____   Zip _____   Telephone No. _____

Relationship to Applicant _____   Relationship to Applicant _____

Employer _____   Telephone No. _____   Employer _____   Telephone No. _____

I. PROMISSORY NOTE FOR A PARENT LOAN GUARANTEED BY NYSHESC

For value received, I the undersigned borrower identified in Part 1A, Item 2, promise to pay my lender or subsequent holder of this promissory note, such loan as advanced in my behalf as identified to me in the Notice of Loan Guarantee and Disclosure Statement plus an amount equivalent to simple interest, as set forth in paragraph III, and any other charges which may become due as provided in paragraph VI. If I fail to pay any of these amounts when they are due, I will pay all charges and other costs, including fees of an outside attorney and court costs that are permitted by federal law and regulations for the collection of this loan, which you incur in collecting this loan (see paragraphs II, III, VI on reverse side). My signature certifies that I have read, understood and agreed to the conditions and authorizations stated in the "Borrower Certification" printed on the reverse side.

I UNDERSTAND THAT THIS IS A PROMISSORY NOTE. I WILL NOT SIGN THIS PROMISSORY NOTE BEFORE READING IT INCLUDING THE WRITING ON THE REVERSE SIDE EVEN IF OTHERWISE ADVISED. I AM ENTITLED TO AN EXACT COPY OF THIS PROMISSORY NOTE, THE NOTICE OF LOAN GUARANTEE AND DISCLOSURE STATEMENT AND ANY AGREEMENT I SIGN. BY SIGNING THIS PROMISSORY NOTE I ACKNOWLEDGE THAT I HAVE RECEIVED AN EXACT COPY HEREOF.

14.
Parent Borrower Signature   Date   MONTH   DAY   YEAR

NOTICE TO BORROWER
Terms of the Promissory Note continue on the reverse side.

PART 1B—TO BE COMPLETED BY STUDENT

PART 1B STUDENT

15. SOCIAL SECURITY NUMBER

16. NAME

Last   First   MI

17. BIRTHDATE

Month   Day   Year

18. STUDENT'S MAJOR COURSE OF STUDY

19. U.S. Citizenship Status
● 1 ☐ Citizen   2 ☐ Eligible Non-citizen
Alien Registration Number

20. Period Covered by this loan
Month   Year   Month   Year
From _____ To _____

21. WHILE IN SCHOOL STUDENT INTENDS TO LIVE (check one)
☐ With Parents   ☐ On campus   ☐ Off campus

22. I have read and understand the terms of the "Student Certification" printed on the REVERSE of this application
Signature of Student: _____

23. Date   MONTH   DAY   YEAR

PART 2—TO BE COMPLETED BY THE SCHOOL

PART 2 SCHOOL

24. NAME OF THE SCHOOL _____

26. ACADEMIC PERIOD OF LOAN (Use Numbers)
Month   Year   Month   Year
● From _____ To _____

25. ADDRESS _____   City _____   State _____   Zip Code _____

27. CLASS YEAR (Check only one)
Undergraduate or equivalent   Graduate or Professional
1 ☐ Fr   2 ☐ So   3 ☐ Jr   4 ☐ Sr   5 ☐ 5yr   6 ☐ 1yr   7 ☐ 2yr   8 ☐ 3yr   9 ☐ 4yr   0 ☐ 5yr

28. FEDERAL SCHOOL CODE

29. AREA CODE/PHONE NO.
( )

● 30. Estimated Cost of Attendance for Loan Period.
$ _____

● 31. Estimated Financial Aid for Loan Period.
$ _____

32. Enrollment Status
1 ☐ Full Time   2 ☐ Half Time

33. I have read and understand the terms of the "School Certification" printed on the REVERSE of this application.

SIGNATURE OF AUTHORIZED SCHOOL OFFICIAL   PRINT OR TYPE NAME AND TITLE

DATE ●   MONTH   DAY   YEAR

PART 3—TO BE COMPLETED BY LENDER

PART 3 LENDER

34. NAME OF LENDER _____

35. ADDRESS _____
City _____   Zip Code _____

36. AREA CODE/PHONE NUMBER (

37. FEDERAL LENDER CODE

38. AMOUNT LENDER APPROVES
● $ _____

39. SIGNATURE OF LENDING OFFICIAL   PRINT OR TYPE NAME AND TITLE
MONTH   DAY   YEAR
DATE

1 ☐   2 ☐   3 ☐   4 ☐   5 ☐   6 ☐

LENDER COPY (ORIGINAL)

Department of Education's borrower responsibilities

Because the Department of Education is very precise in citing its mandates on borrower responsibility and borrower rights, it is best to reprint them here without any changes.

- When you sign a promissory note, you are agreeing to repay according to the terms of the note. This note is a *binding legal document*. This commitment to repay means that, except in cases of cancellation, *you will have to pay back the loan*— even if you don't complete your education, aren't able to get a job after you complete the program, or you're dissatisfied with, or don't receive, the education you paid for. *Think about what this obligation means before you take out a loan.* If you don't pay back your loan on time or according to the terms in your promissory note, you may go into default, which has very serious consequences.
- You must make payments on your loan even if you don't receive a bill. Billing statements (or coupon books) are sent as a convenience, but not receiving them doesn't relieve you of your obligation to make payments.
- You must notify your school/lender if you graduate, withdraw, or drop below half-time status; if you change your name, address, or Social Security Number; or if you transfer to another school.
- Before you receive your first disbursement, you must attend an entrance interview, and before you leave school, you must attend an exit interview.

Department of Education borrower rights

- You have the right to a grace period before your repayment period begins if you have a Perkins or a Stafford Loan. The grace period begins when you leave school or drop below half-time status. The exact length of your grace period is shown on your promissory note.
- You must be given a loan repayment schedule, which lets you know when your first payment is due and the number, frequency, and amount of all payments.
- You must be given a list of deferment and cancellation provisions and the conditions under which the Department of Defense will repay your loan.

- You must be given information about hardship deferments for Perkins Loans and about forbearance for Stafford and PLUS loans.

Before your school gives you your first loan disbursement, your school/lender must give you the following information about your loan(s) in an **entrance interview**:

- The full amount of the loan, the interest rate, and the date you must start repaying.
- The effect borrowing will have on your eligibility for other types of financial aid.
- A complete list of any charges you must pay (loan fees) and information on how those charges are collected.
- The yearly and total amounts you can borrow and the maximum and minimum repayment periods.
- A current description of loans you owe your school/lender, an estimate of your total debt, and an estimate of your monthly payments.
- An explanation of default and its consequences.
- An explanation of options for prepaying your loan at any time without penalty, for refinancing your loan, and for taking advantage of *loan consolidation*.

At an **exit interview** your school/lender must tell you:

- The amount of your total debt (**principal** and **interest**), your interest rate, and the total interest charges on your loan.
- The name of the school/organization that holds your loan, where to send your payments, and where to write if you have questions about your loan.
- What fees you should expect during the repayment period.
- About repayment options such as prepayment, **refinancing**, and **loan consolidation**.

You're entitled to some specific information if you have a Stafford Loan. Your school must:

- Give you general information on the average indebtedness of those who have received Stafford Loans at the school.
- Tell you what your average expected monthly repayment is, based on that average indebtedness.
- Give you debt management advice that the school feels will help you in making your payments.

PLUS Loans

In addition to the financial aid available to help families lower the cost of education, **PLUS Loans** are also available to parents. A PLUS Loan is supposed to make up the financial gap when the school cannot entirely satisfy the family's financial need. A PLUS Loan is a loan to the *parents*, who receive better terms than they would be able to get through a personal loan application .

Unfortunately, each year more and more parents rely on PLUS Loans to bail them out when they can't make tuition payments. Before you apply for a PLUS Loan, please consider all of the following:

Do not apply for a PLUS Loan until after your child has applied for all the *real* financial aid available, and you are aware of what you will receive and what your needs are. Apply only for the amount of money that you will need for the current academic year. These loans require repayment to begin almost at once. If not the principal, you must pay the interest until your children are out of school. Then you must pay back the principal and the interest in monthly payments for up to 10 years.

It is important that you realize that PLUS Loans do not reduce the cost of college. They simply take pressure off and put the responsibility of repayment into the future.

Assess your ability to repay these loans before committing to them. For an approximate amount of repayment costs, figure to repay about $50 per month for each $4,000 that you borrow.

How much will I have to pay each month?

The amount of each payment depends on the size of your debt and on the length of your repayment period. Usually, you'll have to pay at least $50 per month. Ask your lender what your monthly payments will be before you take out the loan. This way you'll know what to expect.

If a parent or student decides to repay the loan ahead of schedule, there is never a penalty charge.

The following chart shows estimated monthly payments based on fixed interest rates of 7%, 8%, 9%, and 10%.

Note: If the total balance of your loan is $4,000 or less, monthly payments must still be at least $50 per month.

The purpose of this chart is to help you estimate the amount of interest that would accrue on your loan every month so that you can estimate how much would be added to your loans principal if you and your lender agree to capitalize interest as described in Paragraphs 6(a) and 9 on the front side of this form.

Approximate
Monthly Accrued Interest
if Interest Rate is:

Principal	6.0%	7.0%	8.0%	9.0%	10.0%	11.0%
$500.00	$2.50	$2.92	$3.33	$3.75	$4.17	$4.58
$1,000.00	$5.00	$5.83	$6.67	$7.50	$8.33	$9.17
$1,500.00	$7.50	$8.75	$10.00	$11.25	$12.50	$13.75
$2,000.00	$10.00	$11.67	$13.33	$15.00	$16.67	$18.33
$2,500.00	$12.50	$14.58	$16.67	$18.75	$20.83	$22.92
$3,000.00	$15.00	$17.50	$20.00	$22.50	$25.00	$27.50
$3,500.00	$17.50	$20.42	$23.33	$26.25	$29.17	$32.08
$4,000.00	$20.00	$23.33	$26.67	$30.00	$33.33	$36.67
$4,500.00	$22.50	$26.25	$30.00	$33.75	$37.50	$41.25
$5,000.00	$25.00	$29.17	$33.33	$37.50	$41.67	$45.83
$5,500.00	$27.50	$32.08	$36.67	$41.25	$45.83	$50.42
$6,000.00	$30.00	$35.00	$40.00	$45.00	$50.00	$55.00
$6,500.00	$32.50	$37.92	$43.33	$48.75	$54.17	$59.58
$7,000.00	$35.00	$40.83	$46.67	$52.50	$58.33	$64.17
$7,500.00	$37.50	$43.75	$50.00	$56.25	$62.50	$68.75

The advantage of capitalizing interest is that you would not be required to make interest payments during any period described in Paragraphs 6(a) and 9. The disadvantage would be that you will pay more in interest charges over the life of your loan because your interest charges will be added to your principal balance. Your monthly repayment amount will be higher if you choose to capitalize.

For example, if you owe $500.00 in principal at an interest rate of 6.0%, then approximately $2.50 in interest would accrue on your loan every month. If you and your lender agree to capitalization on a quarterly basis (every three months), approximately $7.50 would be added to your $500.00 principal balance. As a result, at the end of one quarter you would owe, and interest would accrue on, $507.50 in principal.

Or, if you owe $4,000.00 in principal at an interest rate of 11.0%, then approximately $36.67 in interest would accrue on your loan every month. If you and your lender had agreed to capitalize interest on a quarterly basis (every three months), approximately $110.01 would be added to your $4,000.00 principal balance. As a result, at the end of one quarter, you would owe, and interest would accrue on, $4,110.01 in principal.

Contact your lender if you have questions or need more information.

DEFERMENT SUMMARY: PERKINS LOANS, STAFFORD LOANS, AND PLUS/LOANS

Deferment Condition	Perkins	Stafford	PLUS[1]
Study at a postsecondary school	At least half-time*	Full-time[2] or half-time*[3]	Full-time[2] or half-time*[3]
Study at a school operated by the Federal Government	NO	Full-time only	Full-time only and only for the dependent child
Study in an eligible graduate fellowship program or in a rehabilitation training program for the disabled	NO	YES	YES
Volunteer in Peace Corps, ACTION Programs, or comparable full-time volunteer work for a tax-exempt organization	Up to 3 years each	Up to 3 years each	NO[4]
Active duty member of U.S. armed forces,[5] service in the Commissioned Corps of U.S. Public Health Service, or active duty member of National Oceanic and Atmospheric Administration Corps (NOAAC)[6]	Up to 3 years total	Up to 3 years total	NO[4]
Temporarily totally disabled, or can't work because you're caring for a temporarily totally disabled spouse or other dependent	Up to 3 years ("Other dependent" applies to Perkins Loans only, not to NDSL's)	Up to 3 years	Up to 3 years
Full-time teacher in a public or non-profit private elementary or secondary school in a teacher shortage area as determined by the U.S. Department of Education	NO	Up to 3 years[7]	NO
Eligible internship deferment	Up to 2 years	Up to 2 years	NO[4]
Unemployment	At school's discretion[9]	Up to 2 years	Up to 2 years
Mother of preschool age children, who is going to work (or back to work) at a salary no more than $1.00 over the minimum wage	Up to 1 year[8]	Up to 1 year[7]	NO
Parental leave deferment	Up to 6 months[8]	Up to 6 months	NO
During a period of hardship to the borrower, as determined by the school[9]	YES (also applies to NDSL's)	NO, but see "forbearance"	NO, but see "forbearance"

[1] Deferments are for principal only.
[2] Study must be at a school participating in the Stafford, Plus, and SLS programs.
[3] Half-time* study is allowed only at schools participating in the Stafford, PLUS, and SLS programs, and only for new borrowers* who have a Stafford Loan or an SLS for the current period of enrollment.
[4] ...for all loans made on or after August 15, 1983, but YES for all loans made before that date.
[5] Includes members of the National Guard or Reserves on full-time active duty in the armed forces.
[6] NOAAC deferments are for Perkins Loan borrowers (but not for National Direct/Defense Student Loan [NDSL] borrowers) and for new borrowers* who have a Stafford Loan or an SLS.
[7] For new borrowers* only.
[8] Applies to Perkins Loans only, not to National Direct/Defense Student Loans (NDSL's)
[9] Principal and interest may be deferred, but interest continues to accumulate.

IMPORTANT: PLUS Loan eligibility is based on past credit history.

Parents may now borrow the full cost of a child's college education minus any financial aid. Need is not a factor in the PLUS Loan program.

There is a substantial **origination fee** associated with the PLUS Loan program (6.5% origination fee plus an insurance fee, usually 3%).

Interest Rate

The PLUS Loan has a variable interest rate of 3.1% for the Treasury bill rate with a 10% interest cap.

How does a PLUS borrower apply?

The same way as for a Stafford Loan. Unlike Stafford Loan borrowers, PLUS borrowers do not have to show financial need. However, like all borrowers, they may have to undergo a credit analysis. Note that your school can refuse to certify your loan application, or can certify a loan for an amount less than you would be eligible for.

PLUS Loan applications are available at most banks and lending institutions in addition to your financial aid office.

When do I have to begin repaying these loans?

After the final loan disbursement has been made, PLUS borrowers usually have 60 days to begin repayment of principal and interest. If you have applied for a hardship principal deferment plan, principal can be deferred, and interest only is paid on a monthly basis until you graduate or leave school. Deferments don't apply to *interest*, although the organization holding the loan may let the interest accumulate until the deferment ends.

Statement of Educational Purpose/Certification Statement on Refunds and Default

You must sign this statement in order to receive federal student aid. By signing it, you're stating that you do not owe a refund on a Pell Grant or Supplemental Educational Opportunity Grant (SEOG), that you're not in default on a Perkins Loan, Stafford Loan, or SLS, and the amount you've borrowed under those loan programs doesn't exceed the allowable limits. You're also agreeing to use your student aid only for education-related expenses. Part 1 of the Student Aid Report (SAR) contains such a statement. You must sign either this one or a similar one prepared by your school.

Note: If your parents want to take out a PLUS Loan for you, neither you *nor your parents* can owe a refund or be in default. Your parents will also have to sign a **Statement of Educational Purpose/Certification Statement on Refunds and Default** that your school will prepare.

Statement of Registration Status:

If you're required to register with the Selective Service, you must sign a statement indicating that you have registered before you can receive any federal student aid. This requirement applies to males who were born on or after January 1, 1960, are at least 18, are **citizens** or **eligible non-citizens**, and are not currently on active duty in the armed forces. Citizens of the Federated States of Micronesia, the Marshall Islands, or the Trust Territory of the Pacific [Palau] are exempt from registering.

Part 1 of the Student Aid Report contains a **Statement of Registration Status**. You must sign either that one or a similar one prepared by your school. (Some schools require all students to sign a statement, indicating either that the student has registered with the Selective Service or is not required to do so.)

Before you borrow, ask yourself . . .

How much debt can I afford?

The charts on pages 86 give examples of monthly payments for specific loan amounts. If you plan to apply for student loans each year you're in school, try to estimate how much your monthly payments will be when you leave school. Eventually, the piper must be paid. Of course, if your parents are going to help you pay back these loans, then, perhaps, you should take the maximum allowed, but remember, it's your name that's on the loan.

What if my plans change?

Many unforeseen circumstances can change a student's career goals. The loss of a job or illness in one's family can shift a student's responsibilities and make the repayment of a loan more difficult than originally expected. If you have extenuating circumstances and you have a Perkins Loan or a Stafford Loan, or if your parents have a PLUS Loan, you can write requesting forbearance of the loan holder, but it is wholly up to the lender to forbear or not.

Loan consolidation may also help, because then you are dealing with only one creditor. Many colleges insist that you use the same lender each year in order to avoid confusion and to be in the best situation in case you have to refinance the loan. This will also make it easier if you want to borrow again in the future. For more information on loan consolidation, contact your lender or financial aid administrator.

Borrower beware

There are many organizations with impressive sounding names that will solicit what they call "student loans." In addition to high interest rates, these organizations have many hidden charges, including a fee to look over the application they send you. These lending institutions depend on parents who are uninformed of the federal and state programs that are available. If you are having a problem paying your children's tuition costs, contact the college's financial aid office and find out what state, federal, and school loans are available to you. As far as these other organizations are concerned, my advice is to stay away.

7. GRANTS

Money is also available for financing a college education in the form of grants, many of which are funded by private organizations or industries. There are also two types of federal grants which will enter into your financial aid picture: the **Pell Grant** and the **Supplemental Educational Opportunity Grant (SEOG)**.

Pell Grants

The Pell Grant was once called the Basic Education Opportunity Grant (BEOG), and the man who created, developed and fought for this program was Senator Claiborne Pell of Rhode Island.

Under normal circumstances, 95% of the people reading this book will not be eligible for a Pell Grant. That is because they must have a very low family income to receive a Pell Grant. However, you must show a college that you have been turned down for a Pell Grant before it will consider you for any other types of financial aid, because the information you have supplied in your application for the Pell Grant becomes the criteria for all other financial need judgments which will be made by the financial aid administrator at your college. However, if you are eligible for a Pell Grant, it is free money that does not have to be paid back.

The Pell Grant program is the largest federally funded financial aid program dispersed by the colleges themselves. Cuts in the program are usually highly publicized, giving the impression that there is less and less money available for financial aid. Nothing could be further from the truth. First of all, cuts in the Pell Grant program will have little or no effect on the large majority of people reading this book. However, colleges expect you to apply for a Pell Grant and won't consider giving you *any* other funds until they know the status of your Pell Grant application. Therefore, the denial of a Pell Grant is just as important in the construction of your financial aid package as receiving one. The college wants to know that you've applied to all available sources of financial aid.

Application for the Pell Grant is included in the FAFSA (Free Application For Student Aid). Forms are available at high school and college financial aid offices and public libraries.

What is a Pell Grant?

A Pell Grant is an award to help first-time undergraduates pay for their education after high school. A first-time undergraduate is one who has not earned a bachelor's or first professional degree (a professional degree includes a degree in such fields as pharmacy or dentistry, for example).

Eligibility for those who receive a Pell Grant for the first time is usually limited to five to six years of undergraduate study, not including remedial course work. For many students, Pell Grants provide a foundation of financial aid, to which aid from other federal and non-federal sources may be added.

Pell Grant

Maximum Grant	Academic Year
$3,700	1993-94
$3,900	1994-95
$4,100	1995-96
$4,300	1996-97
$4,500	1997-98

Sounds great doesn't it? What they haven't told you is that although the maximum amount that you can receive has been increased, the amount that you actually receive will be much lower. This is because no additional money has been put into the program. Even though the maximum Pell Grant has been increased to the listings above, the maximum amount that any student will receive is only about $2,100.

How does a student apply for a Pell Grant?

To apply for a Pell Grant, the student must complete one of the following forms:

- The U.S. Department of Education's
  Free Application for Federal Student Aid (FAFSA)

- The American College Testing Program's
  Family Financial Statement (FFS)
- The College Scholarship Service's
  Financial Aid Form (FAF)
- The Pennsylvania Higher Education Assistance Agency's
  Application for Pennsylvania State Grant and Federal Student Aid

The Free Application for Federal Student Aid is a free form and can always be used if the student is only applying for aid from the U.S. Department of Education programs.

Anti-Drug Abuse Act Certification

Some of the language in the **Anti-Drug Abuse Act Certification** is probably a little scary for people who have never contemplated using or distributing drugs. It is also a little silly. After all, if you do use or distribute drugs, you probably will have no scruples about lying when you fill out this report. But the form does exist, and you must fill it out.

To receive a Pell Grant, you must sign a statement certifying that you will not make, distribute, dispense, possess, or use illegal drugs during the period covered by the grant. In addition, you are also certifying that if you are convicted of a drug-related offense committed during that period, you will report the conviction in writing to the U.S. Department of Education. Your Student Aid Report (SAR) will contain this certification statement, although in some cases, your school may ask you to sign a statement it has prepared instead.

Note: Your eligibility for *any* of the programs covered in this book may be suspended or terminated by a court as part of a conviction for possessing or distributing illegal drugs.

Citizen/Eligible Non-Citizen

You must be one of the following to receive federal student aid:
- U.S. citizen
- U.S. national (includes natives of American Samoa or Swain's Island)
- U.S. permanent resident who has an I-151, I-551, or I-551C (Alien Registration Receipt Card)

If you're not in one of these categories, you must have an Arrival-Departure Record (I-94) from the U.S. Immigration and Naturalization Service (INS) showing one of the following designations:

- "Refugee"
- "Asylum Granted"
- "Indefinite Parole" and/or "Humanitarian Parole"
- "Cuban-Haitian Entrant, Status Pending"
- "Conditional Entrant" (valid only if issued before April 1, 1980)
- Other eligible non-citizen with a Temporary Resident Card (I-688)

You're also eligible for federal student aid if you have a suspension of deportation case pending before Congress.

Sometimes the questions of immigrant rights are more complex than the above rules cover. If you feel that you are eligible for financial aid, I advise getting advice from the Department of Immigration or telling your story to your local congressman.

Basic program information

What are the basic eligibility requirements for a Pell Grant?

Here are the eligibility requirements of a Pell Grant as precisely stipulated in the Department of Education's mandates.

To receive a grant, a student must not only demonstrate financial need, but must also meet other basic eligibility requirements. The student must:

- Be enrolled as a regular student in an **eligible program** at an eligible school.
- Have a high school diploma or its recognized equivalent (or be above the age of compulsory school attendance in the state where the school is located and have the ability to benefit from the course of study at the school).
- Be either a U.S. citizen or an eligible non-citizen.
- Be enrolled at least half-time.
- Be making satisfactory progress in his/her course of study.
- Sign a Statement of Updated Information, Registration Status, Anti-Drug Abuse Act Certification, Statement of Educational Purpose, Statement of Refunds and Defaults.

A student is *not* eligible for a Pell Grant if he or she:

- Has a baccalaureate degree.
- Is enrolled in an elementary or secondary school.

- Has borrowed more than the annual or aggregate loan limits for the Department of Education loan programs.
- Has exceeded Pell eligibility limits.
- Is in default on a student loan or owes a refund on a student grant from the U.S. Department of Education.

In addition, if a student transfers from one post-secondary school to another, the student must arrange to have a financial aid transcript sent to the new school by the previous school (or schools, if the student has attended several post secondary schools). The financial aid administrator at the new school will need the information on the financial aid transcript to determine the student's eligibility at that school.

What is a Supplemental Educational Opportunity Grant (SEOG)?

The Supplemental Educational Opportunity Grant is the second of the federal government's grant (free money) programs. It was designed to provide help to first time undergraduates with exceptional financial need, as determined by the college. This money does not need to be repaid. Priority is given to Pell Grant recipients.

How much can I get?

You can get up to $4,000 a year, depending on the restrictions noted on the preceding page.

What's the difference between an SEOG and a Pell Grant?

The Pell Grant program guarantees that if you show eligibility, you will receive a grant. SEOG is a smaller program with limited funds. It is awarded to students based on the discretion of the financial aid administrator at the college. There is no guarantee that even a needy family will receive this grant.

How will I be paid?

You will not touch the money. If the college decides to give you a SEOG grant, they will credit the amount of the grant to your tuition bill. Money rarely ever passes from the college to the student or from the government to the student. The college deals directly with the government, using the forms that you sign. The school does all the paperwork, secures the grant, and then credits it to your account. Credits for grants are usually given twice a year at the beginning of each academic term.

8. OTHER WAYS TO FINANCE A COLLEGE EDUCATION WITHOUT HURTING AID ELIGIBILITY

Creating a college fund for your children through your business, corporation, or personal corporation is perhaps the best way to insure that your children will have the money to afford a quality education at the school of their choice. Whether your business is a sole proprietorship, sub chapter S, PC, or corporation, funding college through the use of a "non-qualified" **pension plan** is perhaps the best way to pay for your child's college education. (Don't let the words "non-qualified" throw you. It only means that the plan is not a standard qualified plan and therefore is not subject to IRS, IRISA, and discrimination rules. This way the money can be distributed to you before you are $59^1/_2$ without penalty.)

If you start your college fund when your children are very young, and can get in 15 years of contributions before college withdrawals begin, it is the best vehicle around.

1. *The mechanics of the College Fund Plan*

The **College Fund Plan** maximizes the personal use of tax deductible corporate dollars. The goal is to use corporate dollars to produce future individual college funds. This is similar to the function of a pension plan, but without all the restrictions and red tape.

As in a pension plan, all payments into the plan are tax deductible to the business or corporation and cash accumulates in the plan without tax. The plan's greatest advantages are that there are no discrimination rules (all employees need not be covered) and that the plan has incredible flexibility (very few rules that govern it) allowing the plan to be custom-tailored. The custom-tailoring decisions extend to:

1. The amounts contributed
2. The age at which an individual stops contributing to the plan
3. The age at which an individual starts to accept funds from the plan
4. How the individual receives the plan disbursements
5. The ability to alter the plan after it has been set in motion

Your business or corporation pays for a special whole life policy which is owned by the employee. The payment is considered income to the employee and is added to the employee's W-2 form. Thus, the payment is tax deductible as employee compensation.

Conversely, the employee's taxable income increases. Uniquely, the plan features a very high, tax free distribution starting in the third year, which is used to offset the income tax due.

When the children reach college age, I suggest a reduced paid up program. The death benefit stays in place for the remainder of the parents' life while continuing to receive an annual distribution.

To summarize, we are able to set a tax deductible, discriminatory college funding plan with tax free growth, which yields tax free funds for college costs and retains a death benefit.

2. Life insurance for college funding

Life insurance has been and still is the absolutely best way to fund a college education. The cash value of an insurance policy is not considered to be an asset when applying for college financial aid. I have clients who have policies with cash values exceeding $300,000, and because these funds are sheltered in an insurance policy, these families are still eligible for college financial aid.

The cash value of an insurance policy increases on a tax deferred basis. This will give you a higher yield than present certificate of deposits or savings accounts, and when your children reach college age you can withdraw the cash value as you need it or borrow against the policy at favorable rates with great tax benefits. If the parent dies, the death benefit will pay for the children's education.

Currently, there are only two legal ways to shelter money so it won't count against you when you apply for financial aid. The first is a **tax deferred annuity** and the second is life insurance.

The tax deferred annuity gives you high interest and tax deferred savings while it doesn't count as an asset for financial aid purposes. Most of these plans have penalties assessed by the insurance company if a withdrawal of more than 10% per year is made in the first seven years. There is also a penalty assessed by the federal government if you withdraw your money before you reach the age of $59^1/_2$. If you set up this account for purposes of receiving college financial aid, the penalties can be small compared to all you will gain.

3. *Sheltering a child's trust*

Moving a child's trust into a single premium insurance deposit will shelter your child's trust while giving a high rate of return. The child becomes the owner and beneficiary of an insurance policy on one of the parents (usually the parent who earns the most money). The only other vehicle for sheltering a trust is the tax deferred retirement account. When all the penalties and restrictions are taken into account, the single premium insurance deposit is the superior product.

If you would like more information on these plans and how these plans can work for you, write to David Jaffe, College Funding Plans, 44-P Jefryn Boulevard, Deer Park, New York 11729.

9. STUDENT AID REPORT (SAR)

After you apply for federal student aid, you'll receive a Student Aid Report (SAR) in approximately four weeks. The SAR will contain the information you gave on your application plus numbers that tell you about your eligibility for federal student aid.

This is your official notification of the results of processing your financial aid form. It contains your expected family contribution number which is the single most important reason for the entire financial aid process. It also confirms the list of colleges that your family contribution number and your other financial information has been sent to. This original document must be signed and submitted to the financial aid office at the college in which you enroll in order to receive payment of your financial aid award. It also informs the schools of your eligibility for a Pell Grant. Since the vast majority of this book's readers will not be eligible for a Pell Grant, please don't think that you have been turned down for financial aid. You must have a very low income to be eligible for a Pell Grant but in order to be eligible for other college programs, you must show that you have applied for a Pell Grant and you have been turned down.

Sometimes I think that the financial aid analysis services try to intimidate you into thinking that the reason for the Student Aid Report is to give you a chance to change your answers in case they were recorded incorrectly or in case you weren't 100% honest. They will tell you that your form has been selected for validation. Don't worry. Everybody's form has been selected for validation. Validation may produce an image of the college police questioning you under a hot spotlight, but I can assure you that all it means is that the colleges would like a signed copy of the parents' and the student's income tax return.

When should the Student Aid Report be submitted to the school?

Most students who are applying for aid as future freshmen have no idea what college they are going to choose when the Student Aid Report arrives. The Student Aid Report should be reviewed for accuracy and put in a safe place until the student is accepted at his or her college of choice and financial aid award letters have been received. At that point, the student must choose a college and send that college the *signed original copy* of the Student Aid Report. In order to qualify for payment of the financial aid award, the college must receive this report.

Understanding your Student Aid Report

When your SAR arrives, you will notice that it contains all of the information that you submitted on your financial aid forms. This allows you to check the information and correct any mistakes. It will also contain the most important number of all, your family contribution (FC). This is the approximate amount that your family can afford to pay for college according to the federal formula. This number is sent to all the colleges that you have applied to along with your other family information, and is the basis for your financial aid package. If your FC is $2,100 or below, you will probably be eligible for a Pell Grant. It is your eligibility for a Pell Grant that determines how many parts your SAR will have.

You may receive a Pell Grant

If your SAR says . . .
You May Receive a Pell Grant
Your SAR will have three parts:

Part 1: Information Summary

Contains instructions to review your SAR to make sure it's correct, and will give you other information about the results of your FAFSA, determining your eligibility for federal student aid. If your SAR says you're eligible for a federal Pell Grant, your school may use the SAR as the basis to pay you. Or, your school may have already received your application information from the federal application processor and may be able to pay you without the SAR. However, it's best to submit your SAR to your school, just in case.

Part 2: Information Review Form.

If any of the information on the form is incorrect, this is the part of the form that you use to correct that information. You correct your SAR by putting the correct information in the column that says "the correct answer is." You must then sign the SAR at the end of part 2 and return it to the financial aid analysis services. In a couple of weeks you will receive a new SAR.

Part 3: Pell Grant Voucher

This is the part of the SAR that verifies that you are eligible for a Pell Grant, and is for the school's use. If no changes are needed on the SAR, this form is sent along with the rest of your SAR to the college of your choice.

If the information on your SAR is correct, submit all three parts of the SAR to your financial aid administrator right away. Your aid administrator will use the information on your SAR to determine the amount of your Pell rant.

If your SAR says...

You're Ineligible for a Pell rant

Your SAR wll have only two parts for you to send on to the college. Being ineligible for a Pell Grant does not mean that you will not receive finanial aid. It means only that a Pell Grant will not be included in your financial aid package. Contact your financial aid administrator. He or she may use the family contribution (FC) number on the SAR to determine whether you're eligible for other federal student aid. If you are, your school will send you a letter telling you the amount and kinds of financial aid you'll get.

If your SAR says...

Your Eligibility Could Not Be Determined

This means that when you filled out your financial aid applications, you left out important information, and as a result, your application could not be put through the federal formula and could not be determined. Make the requested corrections on part 2, sign and return your SAR to the address listed.

If you have any trouble understanding what you're supposed to do after you get your SAR or how you're supposed to make corrections, your financial aid administrator can help you and can answer any questions you have.

To request a copy of your SAR, write to the agency where you sent your student application form: Federal Student Aid Center, PO Box 84, Washington, D.C. 20004.

When you write, make sure you include in your letter your full name, permanent address, Social Security Number, date of birth, and signature.

Make sure your correct address is on file, or you won't receive your duplicate SAR. You can correct your address by writing to the agency where you sent your application, or to the address given above.

The following is a copy of a Student Aid Report.

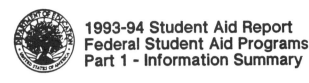

1993-94 Student Aid Report
Federal Student Aid Programs
Part 1 - Information Summary

CCCCC

OMB No. 1840-0132
Form Approved
Exp. 12-31-94

IMPORTANT: Read **ALL** information in Part 1 to find out what to do with this Report.

000245C013

February 02, 1993
EFC: 17714*C

Page 1 of 4

INSTRUCTIONS AND ELIGIBILITY STATUS

This Student Aid Report (SAR) has been produced by   CSS in response to the information you submitted.

This SAR has two parts. Part 1 is the Information Summary. Part 2 is the Information Review Form, which you must use to make any corrections. If all the information on this SAR is correct, you are not eligible to receive a Federal Pell Grant based on the formula we applied to the information on your student aid application. However, you may be eligible for other types of financial aid.

HERE IS WHAT YOU NEED TO DO NOW: Review the information on PART 2. IF ALL THE INFORMATION IS CORRECT, review the Student's Use Box on the back of PART 1. Provide the information required and sign your name. Then submit BOTH PARTS of your SAR to the Financial Aid Administrator (FAA) at the school you plan to attend. He or she will be able to determine your eligibility for aid other than a Federal Pell Grant. IF ANY INFORMATION IS INCORRECT, you may wish to contact your FAA to determine if your school has the ability to correct the SAR electronically. Otherwise, provide the correct answer on PART 2 in the "The correct answer is" column. Sign the Certification at the end of Part 2 and return ONLY PART 2 to the address next to the Certification. Be sure to return BOTH pages of Part 2. (All other parts should be retained for your records.) You will receive a new SAR in about 4 weeks. If you have any questions, contact your FAA.

You provided your parents' estimated 1992 income tax information on your application. If your parents have filed their 1992 income tax return, make the appropriate changes to Section K of this SAR to reflect the information as reported on their return. You can do this by providing the correct information in the "The correct answer is" column on Part 2. If your parents will not have filed an income tax return before you submit your SAR to your school, check with your FAA to find out how to make corrections later, if you need to.

DOCUMENTATION REQUIREMENTS

Your application has been selected for review in a process called verification. You must submit to your school signed copies of certain 1992 financial documents for you and your parents. Contact your FAA to find out which documents are required.

(letter continued on next page)

R4NDN000245 15001300234 C O N N   D
MONTHS   1   2   3   4   5   6   7   8   9   10   11   12
PRIMARY EFC   01968   03936   05904   07872   09840   11808   13776   15744   17714   17828   17942   18056
SECONDARY EFC
TI 00114500; AT 00071170; ST 00014885; IP 00013100; EA 00002500; AI 00043330; NW 0000020200
AP 0000039800; CA 0000002424; AA 00045754; TC 00017714; AC 00017714; SC 00000000; CS 00000000 132-56-2194 RU 01
166 006 150 156 168 170 152 130 169 029 053 002 028 038

This section contains information from your student aid application. Use the Information Review Form (Part 2 of your SAR) to correct this information. Do **not** make corrections on this page.

STUDENT'S INFORMATION

1. LAST NAME		RUIZ
2. FIRST NAME 3. MIDDLE INITIAL		MARLON D
4. PERMANENT STREET ADDRESS	263 WEST END AVENUE	
5. CITY		NEW YORK
6. STATE 7. ZIP CODE		NY 10023
8. STATE OF LEGAL RESIDENCE 9. AS OF		NY (BLANK)
10. SOCIAL SECURITY NUMBER		132-56-2194
11. DATE OF BIRTH		MARCH 07, 1975
12. CITIZENSHIP STATUS		U.S. CITIZEN
13. ALIEN REGISTRATION NUMBER		
14. FIRST BACHELOR'S DEGREE BY 7-1-93?		(BLANK)
15. MARITAL STATUS		UNMARRIED
16. DATE OF MARITAL STATUS		(BLANK)
17. BORN BEFORE 1-1-70?		NO
18. VETERAN OF U.S. ARMED FORCES?		NO
19. GRADUATE/PROFESSIONAL STUDENT?		NO
20. ARE YOU MARRIED?		NO
21. ORPHAN OR WARD OF COURT?		NO
22. HAVE DEPENDENTS OTHER THAN SPOUSE?		NO
23. NUMBER OF FAMILY MEMBERS		DO NOT CORRECT
24. NUMBER IN COLLEGE IN 1993-94		DO NOT CORRECT
25. TYPE OF 1992 TAX FORM USED		NOT FILED
26. EXEMPTIONS CLAIMED		
27. ADJUSTED GROSS INCOME FROM IRS FORM		$
28. U.S. INCOME TAX PAID		$
29. STUDENT'S INCOME EARNED FROM WORK		$
30. SPOUSE'S INCOME EARNED FROM WORK		$
31. ANNUAL SOCIAL SECURITY BENEFITS		$
32. ANNUAL AFDC/ADC		$
33. ANNUAL CHILD SUPPORT RECEIVED		$
34. OTHER UNTAXED INCOME		$
35. MONTHLY VA BENEFITS		$
36. NO. OF MONTHS VA BENEFITS RECEIVED		
37. CASH, SAVINGS, AND CHECKING		$
38. OTHER REAL ESTATE/INVESTMENT VALUE		$
39. OTHER REAL ESTATE/INVESTMENT DEBT		$
40. BUSINESS VALUE		$
41. BUSINESS DEBT		$
42. FARM VALUE		$
43. FARM DEBT		$
44. DOES FAMILY LIVE ON FARM?		(BLANK)
45. UNPAID BALANCE ON STAFFORD LOANS		$
46. UNPAID BAL. ON MOST RECENT STAFFORD		$
47. INTEREST RATE ON MOST RECENT STAFFORD		(BLANK)
48. LOAN PERIOD OF MOST RECENT STAFFORD		(BLANK)
49. CLASS LEVEL FOR MOST RECENT STAFFORD		(BLANK)
50. STUDENT'S PHONE NUMBER		(212) 799-9377
51. DRIVER'S LICENSE NUMBER		R21368946759023475
52. DRIVER'S LICENSE STATE CODE		NY
53. COLLEGE NAME	COLUMBIA UNIVERSITY	
54. COLLEGE CITY AND STATE	NEW YORK, NY	
55. COLLEGE NAME	CORNELL UNIVERSITY	
56. COLLEGE CITY AND STATE	ITHACA, NY	
57. COLLEGE NAME	LAFAYETTE COLLEGE	
58. COLLEGE CITY AND STATE	EASTON, PA	
59. COLLEGE NAME	UNIVERSITY OF ROCHESTER	
60. COLLEGE CITY AND STATE	ROCHESTER, NY	

61. COLLEGE NAME	BRANDEIS UNIVERSITY	
62. COLLEGE CITY AND STATE	WALTHAM, MA	
63. COLLEGE NAME		
64. COLLEGE CITY AND STATE		
65. SHOULD DATA BE RELEASED TO STATE?		YES
66. SIGNED BY		BOTH
67. DATE SIGNED		JANUARY 18, 1993
68. PREPARER'S SSN		(BLANK)
69. PREPARER'S EIN		(BLANK)
70. PREPARER'S SIGNATURE		(BLANK)

STATE INFORMATION

71. FATHER'S GRADE LEVEL COMPLETED		COLLEGE
72. MOTHER'S GRADE LEVEL COMPLETED		COLLEGE
73. DIPLOMA TYPE 74. DIPLOMA DATE		H.S. GRAD. 05/93
75. ATTENDING SAME COLLEGE IN 1993-94?		(BLANK)
76. ENROLLMENT STATUS FOR SUMMER '93		(BLANK)
77. ENROLLMENT STATUS FOR FALL '93		FULL TIME
78. ENROLLMENT STATUS FOR WINTER '94		(BLANK)
79. ENROLLMENT STATUS FOR SPRING '94		(BLANK)
80. DEGREE/CERT. 81. COURSE OF STUDY		BA LA
82. DATE EXPECTED TO COMPLETE PROGRAM		05/97
83. YEAR IN COLLEGE IN 1993-94		1ST
84. STUDENT'S HOUSING STATUS		CAMPUS
85. CHILD CARE PAID FOR HOW MANY CHILDREN		
86. DATE APPLICATION RECEIVED		JANUARY 26, 1993

PARENTS' INFORMATION

87. MARITAL STATUS		MARRIED
88. STATE OF LEGAL RESIDENCE 89. AS OF		NY (BLANK)
90. NUMBER OF FAMILY MEMBERS		03
91. NUMBER IN COLLEGE IN 1993-94		1
92. TYPE OF 1992 TAX FORM USED		ESTIMATED 1040
93. EXEMPTIONS CLAIMED		03
94. ADJUSTED GROSS INCOME FROM IRS FORM		$ 114,500
95. U.S. INCOME TAX PAID		$ 32,319
96. FATHER'S INCOME EARNED FROM WORK		$ 53,000
97. MOTHER'S INCOME EARNED FROM WORK		$ 60,000
98. ANNUAL SOCIAL SECURITY BENEFITS		$
99. ANNUAL AFDC/ADC		$
100. ANNUAL CHILD SUPPORT RECEIVED		$
101. OTHER UNTAXED INCOME		$
102. AGE OF OLDER PARENT		48
103. CASH, SAVINGS, AND CHECKING		$ 20,000
104. OTHER REAL ESTATE/INVESTMENT VALUE		$ 54,000
105. OTHER REAL ESTATE/INVESTMENT DEBT		$ 14,000
106. BUSINESS VALUE		$ 0
107. BUSINESS DEBT		$ 0
108. FARM VALUE		$ 0
109. FARM DEBT		$ 0
110. DOES FAMILY LIVE ON FARM?		NO

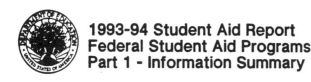

1993-94 Student Aid Report
Federal Student Aid Programs
Part 1 - Information Summary

CCCCC

OMB No. 1840-0132
Form Approved
Exp. 12-31-94

-01 PIN: 0002

IMPORTANT: Read **ALL** information in Part 1 to find out what to do with this Report.

(letter continued)

SPECIAL COMMENTS

Your registration or your exemption status has been confirmed by Selective Service.

To receive Federal student aid, you cannot be in default on any Department of Education student loan. We were unable to determine whether you are in default. Contact your FAA for more information.

If you have special circumstances that might affect the amount you and your family are expected to contribute toward your education, see your Financial Aid Administrator (FAA).

We estimate that it will take you approximately 30-45 minutes to review and complete this SAR. This includes time for reviewing instructions, gathering records, and making corrections to your SAR, if needed. If you have comments about this estimate or suggestions for improving the SAR, send your comments (NOT THE SAR!) to the U.S. Department of Education, Information Management and Compliance Division, Washington, D.C. 20202-4651, or to the Office of Management and Budget, Paperwork Reduction Project (1840-0132), Washington, D.C. 20503.

WARNING: As more fully set forth in Section 5301 of the Anti-Drug Abuse Act of 1988, if you are convicted of drug distribution or possession, your eligibility for Title IV student financial aid is subject to suspension or termination.

R4NDN000245 15001300234 C D [N] N   D
MONTHS   1   2   3   4   5   6   7   8   9   10   11   12
PRIMARY EFC   01968   03936   05904   07872   09840   11808   13776   15744   17714   17828   17942   18056
SECONDARY EFC
TI 00114500; AT 00071170; ST 00014885; IP 00013100; EA 00002500; AI 00043330; NW 0000020200
AP 0000039800; CA 0000002424; AA 00045754; TC 00017714; AC 00017714; SC 00000000; CS 00000000 132-56-2194 RU 01
166 006 150 156 168 170 152 130 169 029 053 002 028 038

We asked for	You told us	The correct answer is

F. Student's Asset Information

	We asked for	You told us		The correct answer is
37.	Cash, Savings, and Checking	$	37	$ .00
38.	Other Real Estate/Investment Value	$	38	$ .00
39.	Other Real Estate/Investment Debt	$	39	$ .00
40.	Business Value	$	40	$ .00
41.	Business Debt	$	41	$ .00
42.	Farm Value	$	42	$ .00
43.	Farm Debt	$	43	$ .00
44.	Does Family Live on Farm?	(BLANK)	44	☐ Yes ☐ No

G. Federal Stafford Loan (GSL) Information

	We asked for	You told us		The correct answer is
45.	Unpaid Balance on Stafford Loans	$	45	$ .00
46.	Unpaid Bal. on Most Recent Stafford	$	46	$ .00
47.	Interest Rate on Most Recent Stafford	(BLANK)	47	
48.	Loan Period of Most Recent Stafford	(BLANK)	48	
49.	Class Level for Most Recent Stafford	(BLANK)	49	
50.	Student's Phone Number	(212) 799-9377	50	- -
51.	Driver's License Number	R21368946759023475	51	.
52.	Driver's License State Code	NY	52	

H. College Release and Certification

	We asked for	You told us		The correct answer is
53.	College Name	COLUMBIA UNIVERSITY	53	
54.	College City and State	NEW YORK, NY	54	
55.	College Name	CORNELL UNIVERSITY	55	
56.	College City and State	ITHACA, NY	56	
57.	College Name	LAFAYETTE COLLEGE	57	
58.	College City and State	EASTON, PA	58	
59.	College Name	UNIVERSITY OF ROCHESTER	59	
60.	College City and State	ROCHESTER, NY	60	
61.	College Name	BRANDEIS UNIVERSITY	61	
62.	College City and State	WALTHAM, MA	62	
63.	College Name		63	
64.	College City and State		64	
65.	Should Data be Released to State?	YES	65	DO NOT CORRECT
66.	Signed By	BOTH	66	DO NOT CORRECT
67.	Date Signed	JANUARY 18, 1993	67	DO NOT CORRECT
68.	Preparer's SSN	(BLANK)	68	- -
69.	Preparer's EIN	(BLANK)	69	-
70.	Preparer's Signature	(BLANK)	70	DO NOT CORRECT

132-56-2194 RU 01

Part 2 (your Information Review Form) is continued on the following page. Please refer to the instructions on the front of Part 2 when reviewing the rest of your information. If you make corrections, send BOTH pages of Part 2 to the address next to the Certification statement at the end of Part 2.

CCCCC

OMB No. 1840-0132
Form Approved
Exp. 12-31-94

1993-94 Student Aid Report
Federal Student Aid Programs
Part 2 - Information Review Form

Processed: 02-02-93
EFC: 17714＊C

- Pay special attention to any items in **BOLDFACE TYPE**; they may need to be corrected.
- To correct an item, print the correct answer in the "The correct answer is" column.
- If you make corrections, send **BOTH pages of Part 2** to the address on the back of Part 2.
  Do not attach tax or any other forms.

-01 PIN: 0002

We asked for	You told us	The correct answer is

A. Student's Information

	We asked for	You told us		The correct answer is
1.	Last Name	RUIZ	1	
2.	First Name 3. Middle Initial	MARLON D	2	3. M.I.
4.	Permanent Street Address	263 WEST END AVENUE	4	
5.	City	NEW YORK	5	
6.	State 7. ZIP Code	NY 10023	6	7. ZIP Code
8.	State of Legal Residence 9. As of	NY (BLANK)	8	9. As of - -
10.	Social Security Number	132-56-2194	10	
11.	Date of Birth	MARCH 07, 1975	11	- -
12.	Citizenship Status	U.S. CITIZEN	12	
13.	Alien Registration Number		13 A	
14.	First Bachelor's Degree by 7-1-93?	(BLANK)	14	☐ Yes ☐ No
15.	Marital Status	UNMARRIED	15	
16.	Date of Marital Status	(BLANK)	16	-

B. Student's Status

		You told us		The correct answer is
17.	Born Before 1-1-70?	NO	17	☐ Yes ☐ No
18.	Veteran of U.S. Armed Forces?	NO	18	☐ Yes ☐ No
19.	Graduate/Professional Student?	NO	19	☐ Yes ☐ No
20.	Are you Married?	NO	20	☐ Yes ☐ No
21.	Orphan or Ward of Court?	NO	21	☐ Yes ☐ No
22.	Have Dependents Other Than Spouse?	NO	22	☐ Yes ☐ No

C. Student's Household Information

		You told us		
23.	Number of Family Members	DO NOT CORRECT	23	
24.	Number in College in 1993-94	DO NOT CORRECT	24	

D. Student's 1992 Income and Benefits

		You told us		The correct answer is
25.	Type of 1992 Tax Form Used	NOT FILED	25	
26.	Exemptions Claimed		26	
27.	Adjusted Gross Income From IRS Form	$	27	$ .00
28.	U.S. Income Tax Paid	$	28	$ .00
29.	Student's Income Earned From Work	$	29	$ .00
30.	Spouse's Income Earned From Work	$	30	$ .00
31.	Annual Social Security Benefits	$	31	$ .00
32.	Annual AFDC/ADC	$	32	$ .00
33.	Annual Child Support Received	$	33	$ .00
34.	Other Untaxed Income	$	34	$ .00

E. Student's Veterans Benefits

		You told us		The correct answer is
35.	Monthly VA Benefits	$	35	$ .00
36.	No. of Months VA Benefits Received		36	

R4NDN000245 15001300234 C D N N   D
MONTHS   1   2   3   4   5   6   7   8   9   10   11   12
PRIMARY EFC   01968 03936 05904 07872 09840 11808 13776 15744 17714 17828 17942 18056
SECONDARY EFC
TI 00114500; AT 00071170; ST 00014885; IP 00013100; EA 00002500; AI 00043330; NW 0000020200
AP 0000039800; CA 0000002424; AA 00045754; TC 00017714; AC 00017714; SC 00000000; CS 00000000 132-56-2194 RU 01

1993-94 Student Aid Report
Federal Student Aid Programs
Part 2 - Information Review Form

CCCCC

OMB No. 1840-0132
Form Approved
Exp. 12-31-94

Processed: 02-02-93
EFC: 17714*C

CONTINUED

Continue reviewing this form as instructed on the previous page.
Be sure to read the information on the back of this page.

-01 PIN: 0002

We asked for	You told us	The correct answer is

I. State Information

RUIZ, MARLON D

We asked for	You told us		The correct answer is
71. Father's Grade Level Completed	COLLEGE	71	
72. Mother's Grade Level Completed	COLLEGE	72	
73. Diploma Type	H.S. GRAD.	73	☐ HIGH SCHOOL ☐ GED
74. Diploma Date	05/93	74	-
75. Attending Same College in 1993-94?	(BLANK)	75	☐ Yes ☐ No
76. Enrollment Status for Summer '93	(BLANK)	76	
77. Enrollment Status for Fall '93	FULL TIME	77	
78. Enrollment Status for Winter '94	(BLANK)	78	
79. Enrollment Status for Spring '94	(BLANK)	79	
80. Degree/Cert. 81. Course of Study	BA LA	80	81.
82. Date Expected to Complete Program	05/97	82	-
83. Year in College in 1993-94	1ST	83	
84. Student's Housing Status	CAMPUS	84	
85. Child Care Paid for How Many Children		85	
86. Date Application Received	JANUARY 26, 1993	86	DO NOT CORRECT

J. Parents' Household Information

We asked for	You told us		The correct answer is
87. Marital Status	MARRIED	87	
88. State of Legal Residence 89. As of	NY (BLANK)	88	89. As of - -
90. Number of Family Members	03	90	
91. Number in College in 1993-94	1	91	

K. Parents' 1992 Income and Benefits

We asked for	You told us		The correct answer is
92. Type of 1992 Tax Form Used	ESTIMATED 1040	92	
93. Exemptions Claimed	03	93	
94. Adjusted Gross Income From IRS Form	$ 114,500	94	$ .00
95. U.S. Income Tax Paid	$ 32,319	95	$ .00
96. Father's Income Earned From Work	$ 53,000	96	$ .00
97. Mother's Income Earned From Work	$ 60,000	97	$ .00
98. Annual Social Security Benefits	$	98	$ .00
99. Annual AFDC/ADC	$	99	$ .00
100. Annual Child Support Received	$	100	$ .00
101. Other Untaxed Income	$	101	$ .00

R4NDN000245 15001300234 C 0 [N] N   D

MONTHS	1	2	3	4	5	6	7	8	9	10	11	12
PRIMARY EFC	01968	03936	05904	07872	09840	11808	13776	15744	17714	17828	17942	18056

SECONDARY EFC
TI 00114500; AT 00071170; ST 00014885; IP 00013100; EA 00002500; AI 00043330; NW 0000020200
AP 0000039800; CA 0000002424; AA 00045754; TC 00017714; AC 00017714; SC 00000000; CS 00000000 132-56-2194 RU 01

We asked for	You told us	The correct answer is

L. Parents' Asset Information

102. Age of Older Parent	48	102 [ ]
103. Cash, Savings, and Checking	$ 20,000	103 $ .00
104. Other Real Estate/Investment Value	$ 54,000	104 $ .00
105. Other Real Estate/Investment Debt	$ 14,000	105 $ .00
106. Business Value	$ 0	106 $ .00
107. Business Debt	$ 0	107 $ .00
108. Farm Value	$ 0	108 $ .00
109. Farm Debt	$ 0	109 $ .00
110. Does Family Live on Farm?	NO	110 ☐ Yes ☐ No

IF YOU MADE NO CHANGES
• complete the STUDENT'S USE
  BOX on Part 1 of your SAR
• submit ALL parts of your SAR to the
  school you plan to attend. Do NOT
  send your SAR to either address
  given on this page.

IF YOU NEED ANOTHER COPY OF YOUR SAR
• write to Federal Student Aid Programs
  P.O. Box 7425
  London, KY 40742-7425

• include your name, social security number and
  signature.

IF YOU MADE CHANGES
• read and sign the Certification
  statement to the right
• send BOTH pages of Part 2 to:

  Federal Student Aid Programs
  P.O. Box 7424
  London, KY 40742-7424

CERTIFICATION
All of the information on this SAR is true and complete to
the best of my knowledge. If I am asked, I agree to
give proof that my information is correct. This proof might
include a copy of the 1992 U.S. Income Tax Form filed
by me or my family. I understand that if I purposely give
false or misleading information on this SAR, I may be
subject to a $10,000 fine, a prison sentence, or both.

STUDENT_____ DATE _____

PARENT_____ DATE _____

Analyzing the Student Aid Report

The SAR on the preceding pages was received by a family of three earning in excess of $144,500 per year. Cash and real estate investment total $60,000 in addition to the $150,000 of equity that they have in their home (value not listed).

Most people would think that this family is too wealthy to receive college aid, but that is not right. The family's contribution number, located under the date in the upper right corner of p. 1 of the SAR, indicates that according to the federal formula, this family can afford to pay $17, 714 per year for college costs. Since the costs of education at some of the colleges that they have applied to are as much as $24,000 per year, they are eligible for over $6,000 in financial aid at these schools **(cost of education *minus* family contribution *equals* eligibility)**.

The only mistake that this family made was not having one of the parents also plan to attend college. Had they done so, this family would have been eligible for over $12,000 in financial aid. Now, being eligible doesn't guarantee that this family will receive financial aid; however, since these colleges are competing with each other for this student, it is very likely that they all will come up with some sort of financial aid package to entice this student to attend their institutions. This Student Aid Report is an encouraging document because most families earning this amount of income would not even bother to apply for financial aid.

10. HOW TO NEGOTIATE WITH THE FINANCIAL AID ADMINISTRATOR

You've done it. The forms are completed and mailed. You've received your Student Aid Report (SAR) confirming that the colleges have received your financial aid information and now, at last, your financial aid award letters begin to arrive . . .

Respond to the financial aid award letter even if you are not sure that you will be attending the college from which it came. You can accept or reject any part of a financial aid package, and you may also appeal for more funds or a change in the composition that the funds have been offered to you (asking for fewer loans and more grants, for example). The only part of a financial aid package that I recommend rejecting is a PLUS or SLS Loan. These loans are no bargains and any college that actually puts these loans into a financial aid package and tries to give you the impression that they are "giving you something" is not.

If you do plan to appeal for more funds, do it right away while there is still money in the school's financial budget. If you wait, you're only making it easy for the college to say, "Sorry, we've run out of money." When stating your case with the financial aid administrator (FAA), stick to the facts and don't look for sympathy. Consider yourself to be a valuable asset to the college. Remember, the college must fill *all* the seats in a classroom in order to operate profitably. Some of these seats are paying full tuition, some are paying half, and some are paying less than half, but just like the airline industry, it doesn't pay to take off with any empty seats.

Although a face-to-face personal appeal is best, this is usually the option only when you are applying to a local college. In most instances, a written appeal stating all of the facts should be sent and a follow-up phone call should be made to the college financial aid office about two weeks later. Remember, when it comes to appealing for more financial aid, it never hurts to ask. Most colleges will bend over backwards to sign up freshmen because they know that they are competing with other schools. After the freshman year, it is much more difficult to successfully appeal for more financial aid funds. The colleges are not competing with other colleges and they know that in all probability you won't transfer or drop out. As an incoming student, you are in the best negotiating position that you will be in for the next four years.

One bargaining plea that you should *not* use, however, is **consumer debt**. The financial aid administrator will not be sympathetic as consumer debt has no weight when it comes to deciding on the size of your financial aid package.

If you own a home or property, the thing to do is to take an **equity loan** to pay off your consumer debt. The interest on the money owed will be smaller and by taking the loan, you are lowering the equity in your property and therefore increasing your eligibility for financial aid. In addition, your cost of interest may be tax deductible. See your accountant to be sure.

Note: Even though your home equity is not a factor in the federal financial aid formula, most private colleges will still take your home equity into consideration when awarding financial aid.

What about next year?

Will my financial aid package be the same in my sophomore, junior, and senior years?

The answer to this question depends on many factors. Since family and financial situations might change or the number of family members attending college might change, you must fill out a new financial aid form each year. If your family's financial situation stays about the same and you continue to be a desirable student, the chances are very good that you will receive similar financial aid packages in your second, third, and fourth years.

However, if the college that you are attending is not considered to be financially sound, there is reason to worry. Some colleges will give exceptional financial aid packages to incoming freshmen as an inducement to sign up. However, after the freshman year has ended, these colleges may scale back your financial aid package in order to have funds to once again give a potential freshman an incentive to enroll.

The senior year

The last financial aid form for undergraduate studies is filed in the spring of the student's junior year. Once that form has been filed, the student is free to get a good summer job (one that might pay a lot of money) without the worry of it being detrimental to his or her financial aid. However, if the student plans to go on to graduate school, the money earned during the senior year *will* have an affect on graduate school financial aid. This is because the senior year at college becomes the first base income year for graduate school. As you can see, this is one of the flaws of the congressional formula. It gives students little incentive to go out and earn money to help pay for their college education.

Whether or not you're happy with your financial aid package, it's always a good idea to ask for more. Even if you don't get it, having a request for more aid on file may prevent having your aid reduced in your sophomore, junior, or senior year.

Since registering freshmen are the life-blood of a college or university, taking aid money from sophomores, juniors, and seniors in order to give a qualified freshman applicant an incentive is not unheard of.

The following are the financial aid packages for the same student in his freshman and senior year. As you can see, the total cost of college increased $4,030 from the freshman year to the senior year. However, at the same time the amount of financial aid was increased to *almost* match the difference. Although the cost of college increased $4,030, costs to the family increased only $1,525.

Note: It may look as though he received an extra $4,000 in his senior year package but the additional $4,000 in aid listed is in the form of a PLUS Loan which is not really financial aid.

Of course, everybody's situation is different. No two case studies are exactly the same, but by going over these packages you'll get a realistic idea of just how these packages are laid out, and have a real understanding of just what you're being offered when your financial aid package arrives.

SYRACUSE UNIVERSITY
OFFICE OF STUDENT FINANCIAL AID
200 ARCHBOLD / SYRACUSE, NEW YORK 13244-1140 / (315) 443-1513

1992 - 1993 AWARD NOTICE

06/10/92
076-72-1933

JOHN Q. STUDENT
MAIN STREET
USA

Syracuse University is pleased to award you the following financial aid:

Accept	Decline	Program	Fall	Spring	Summer	Total
☑	☐	SYRACUSE GRANT	1,540	1,540	0	3,080
☑	☐	S. E. O. G.	750	750	0	1,500
☑	☐	COLLEGE WORK STUDY	1,000	1,000	0	2,000
☐	☐					
☐	☐					
☐	☐					
☐	☐					

Total Syracuse University Financial Aid: **6,580**

Other sources of aid.
3,575 TAP	4,000 PLUS LOAN
2,400 PELL GRANT	4,000 STAFFORD LOAN

Total of other sources of aid: **(These amounts are estimated.)** **13,975**

GRAND TOTAL Syracuse University and other aid: **20,555**

Estimated Cost of Attendance: **21,390**

An explanation of this amount is found in the booklet, *Your Financial Aid Award* under "Billing and Payment Procedures." Bursar Billing information is described in this section.

All aid is subject to change if additional data requested conflicts with information originally submitted on your Financial Aid Form (FAF). Please read carefully the enclosed 1992-93 instruction booklet, *Your Financial Aid Award* **from Syracuse University.**

Christopher Walsh
Director, Financial Aid Services

INSTRUCTIONS: Accept or Decline each form of Syracuse University Financial Aid listed above.
Return this letter by **07/01/92**

SPECIAL NOTICES

STUDENT COPY - RETAIN THIS COPY FOR YOUR RECORDS

L1518

SYRACUSE UNIVERSITY
Financial Aid Award

1991 - 1992

05/23/91
076-72-1933

JOHN Q. STUDENT
MAIN STREET
USA

The estimated cost of attendance for the 1991-92 academic year is: **20,080**

This amount includes tuition and fees, and estimates for housing, meal plan, books, supplies, travel and personal expenses. However, this is not the amount you will be billed. The amount billed will include the actual tuition, fees, housing, and meal plan costs.

Syracuse University is pleased to award you the following financial aid:

Accept	Decline	Program	Fall	Spring	Summer	Total
☐	☐	**SYRACUSE GRANT**	1,540	1,540	0	3,080
☐	☐	**S. E. O. G.**	750	750	0	1,500
☐	☐	**COLLEGE WORK STUDY**	1,000	1,000	0	2,000
☐	☐					
☐	☐					
☐	☐					
☐	☐					

Total Syracuse University Financial Aid: **6,580**

Other sources of aid. (These amounts are estimated):
3,458 TAP   2,400 PELL GRANT
4,000 STAFFORD LOAN

Total of other sources of aid: **9,858**

GRAND TOTAL Syracuse University and other aid: **16,438**

Estimated Student/Family Responsibility: **3,642**
This amount is the difference between the estimated cost of attendance and the total financial aid award.
A COPY OF STUDENT/PARENT 1990 FORM 1040 IS REQUIRED. NON-FILERS MUST SIGN A STATEMENT OF TOTAL INCOME FOR 1990 AND STATE THAT A FORM 1040 HAS NOT AND WILL NOT BE FILED.

All aid is subject to change if additional data requested conflicts with information originally submitted on your Financial Aid Form (FAF). Please read carefully the enclosed 1991-92 instruction booklet, *Your Financial Aid Award* from Syracuse University.

Christopher Walsh
Director, Financial Aid Services

Instructions:
1. Accept or decline each form of Syracuse University Financial Aid listed above.
2. Sign the acceptance agreement below.
3. Return this letter by **06/07/91**
4. Retain the "student copy" for your records.

Acceptance Agreement
I have read and understand this financial aid award notice and the enclosed financial aid award information. I agree to all of the terms and provisions of the award. Failure to comply with any of these terms and provisions could jeopardize this offer and future requests for financial aid from Syracuse University.

Signature _____   Date _____

STUDENT COPY - RETAIN THIS COPY FOR YOUR RECORDS

L165

Breakdown of the two financial aid packages illustrated

Freshman Financial Aid Package

Total Cost of Attendance $17,360

Financial Aid Package:
College Grant $2,800
Supplementary Educational Opportunity Grant $1,500
College Work-Study $1,800
Perkins Loan $1,400
Tuition Assistance Program (state grant) $2,775
Pell Grant $1,150
Guaranteed Student Loan (Stafford Loan) $2,625
Total Grants (free money) $8,225
Total Loans $4,025
Total Financial Aid Package $14,050

Family Contribution $3,310

The Same Student Three Years Later Entering His Senior Year
Senior Financial Aid Package

Total Cost of Attendance $21,390

Financial Aid Package:
College Grant $3,080
Supplemental Educational Opportunity Grant $1,500
College Work-Study $2,000
Tuition Assistance Program (state grant) $3,575
Pell Grant $2,400
Stafford Loan $4,000
PLUS Loan (not really aid) $4,000
Total Grants (free money) $10,555
Total Loans (excluding PLUS Loan) $4,000
Total Financial Aid Package $16,555

Family Contribution $4,835

11. FINANCIAL AID AWARD LETTERS

The real value of grants

$10,000 in grants equals $15,000 in earned income.
Note: This illustration assumes a 35% tax bracket.

Since tuition must be paid with earnings that you have already paid tax on, for each $65 that you pay in tuition costs you must earn $100. What this means put into a large equation is that you must earn $30,000 in income to pay $20,000 in tuition. This tax bite that decreases the value of your earned dollar *increases* the value of any grant or scholarship that you receive. Therefore, $10,000 in grants represents $15,000 if you had to go out and earn that money yourself.

A note about extenuating circumstances

The loss of a job or income, death or illness, the separation or divorce of your parents, or any extenuating circumstance relative to your family's finances should be reported in writing to your college financial aid administrator. If your family has tuition expenses at an elementary or secondary school, let the college know about them.

Although high medical costs and being classified as a dislocated worker are no longer factors in the congressional formula to determine your eligibility for financial aid, Congress has instructed the financial aid administrators at the colleges to take such non-factors into account when awarding financial aid packages. The financial aid administrators are free to use their own discretion. FAAs have the power to adjust your financial aid package, but be prepared to show proof in the form of a doctor's or lawyer's letter confirming the situation. Even if it is too late to help you in your present year, it lets them know that you may be needing help next year.

Who qualifies as a dislocated worker?

Dislocated worker means a person who has been given this classification by the appropriate state agency (such as the state Employment Service or Job Service) in accordance with Title III of the Job Training Partnership Act of 1982 (Public Law 97-300). Generally, the state agency determines a person to be a dislocated worker if the person:

- has been fired or laid off,
- has been laid off as a result of permanent closure of a plant or other facility,

or

- was self-employed (including farmers) but is now unemployed because of poor economic conditions in the community or a natural disaster.

GLOSSARY OF IMPORTANT TERMS

Accelerated Program

A condensed college program that allows the student to cram four years of credits into three or three-and-a-half years. Although it is not recommended for the vast majority of students, it is certainly a way to cut college costs.

American College Testing (ACT)

A financial aid analysis service.

Anti-Drug Abuse Act Certification

A statement that you must sign in order to receive a Pell Grant. This statement is an agreement that you will not make, distribute, disperse, possess, or use illegal drugs during the period covered by the grant. It also requires you to report in writing any conviction of a drug-relate offense committed during the grant period to the U.S. Department of Education.

Assets

Cash, property, investments. Anything that is owned and worth money.

Base Income Year

The year that your family's financial aid package is based on. It begins January 1 of your child's *junior* year of high school and ends December 31 of your child's *senior* year of high school.

Business/Farm Supplement

A supplementary form required by some schools prior to granting a financial aid package. This form is required in order to clarify your business net worth when you are self-employed or own your own business or farm.

Capital Gain

The increase in value of an asset such as stock or real estate between the time that it is bought and the time that it is sold.

Certification Statement on Refunds and Default

A statement that you must sign before you may receive federal financial aid. By signing this statement, you are attesting that you do not owe a refund on a Pell Grant or SEOG, that you are not in default on another student loan, and that the amounts you have borrowed are not in excess of the allowable limits.

College Fund Plan

A plan for funding your child's college education that maximizes the personal use of tax deductible corporate dollars. Similar to a pension plan, all payments are tax deductible by the contributing business or corporation, and cash accumulates without taxes.

College Scholarship Service (CSS)

A financial aid analysis service.

College Work-Study (CWS)

A federal job program (usually on campus) that provides over 80% of the funds for student jobs. In order to qualify for College Work-Study, you must show financial need.

Commercial Property Index

A government index used to determine the current monetary value of your commercial property. The index generally figures a conservative rate of appreciation for the property, based on the year in which the property was purchased.

Congressional Formula

The formula used by the financial aid services to calculate the family contribution.

Consumer Debt

Debt to a lending institution incurred for the purchase of consumer goods.

Custodial Parent

The parent with legal and financial responsibililty for a child, or with whom the child spends the majority of his or her time.

Cost of Education (or Cost of Attendance)

The total amount it will cost a student to go to school — usually expressed as a yearly figure. The cost of education covers tuition and fees; on-campus room and board (or a housing and food allowance for off-campus students); and allowances for books, supplies, transportation, child care, costs related to a handicap, and miscellaneous expenses. Talk to the financial aid administrator at the school you're planning to attend if you have any unusual expenses that may affect your cost of education or your ability to pay that cost.

Note: Cost of Attendance minus Financial Aid equals What You Will Have to Pay. This is the actual family contribution.

Default

Failure to repay a student loan according to the terms agreed to when you signed a promissory note. Default also means failure to submit requests for deferment or cancellation on time. If you default on a student loan, your school, the organization that holds your loan, the state and federal governments all can take action to recover the money — including notifying national credit bureaus of your default. This may affect your future credit rating for a long time. For example, you may find it very difficult to borrow from a bank to buy a car or a house. Also, you may be liable for expenses incurred in collecting the loan. If you decide to return to school, you're not entitled to receive any more federal student aid. Also, the Internal Revenue Service may withhold your income tax refund, and the amount of your refund will be applied toward the amount you owe.

Deferment

Postponement of repayment of your financial aid. Deferment applies only to the principal of a loan, not to the interest accrued on a loan. You must apply for a deferment using a request form obtained from your school.

Dislocated Worker

Status granted an individual according to extenuating circumstances under which your financial aid package may be adjusted or repayment may be deferred. The classification is granted by a state agency if you have been laid off, laid off as a result of the permanent closure of a plant or other facility, or were self-employed but are now unemployed because of the community's economic conditions or a natural disaster (this extends to farmers).

Divorced/Separated Parent's Statement

A supplementary financial aid form required by some colleges prior to the determination of your financial aid package. This form is used to supply information regarding the non-custodial parent's finances and his or her financial responsibility for the child.

Early Decision

A plan offered to applicants who are sure they want to attend a particular school, and are also fairly sure that they will be accepted to that school. Students are usually notified as to acceptance before December 15th of their senior year of high school. Early decision usually requires students not to apply to any other colleges, and because the college isn't competing against other schools for the student, it can also mean receiving an inferior financial aid package.

Eligible Non-citizen

You are considered an eligible non-citizen if you are a U.S. national (including natives of American Samoa or Swain's Island, a U.S. permanent resident with an I-151, I-551, or an I-551C, or if you possess an Arrival-Departure Record (I-94) from the U.S. Immigration and Naturalization Service. The status of eligible non-citizen means that you may receive government financial aid.

Eligible Program

A course of study leading to a degree or certificate at a school participating in one or more of the student aid programs described in this book. To get a Pell Grant, SEOG, Perkins Loan, or a College Work-Study job, you must be enrolled in an eligible program. The same is true for the Stafford, PLUS, or SLS Loan programs, with two exceptions:
- If a school has told you that you must take certain course work to qualify for admission into one of its eligible programs, you can get a

Stafford Loan or an SLS (or your parents can get a PLUS for you) for up to 12 consecutive months while you're completing that course work. You must be enrolled at least *half-time*, and you must meet the usual student aid eligibility requirements.

- If you're enrolled at least *half-time* in a program to obtain a professional credential or certification required by a state for employment as an elementary or secondary school teacher, you can get a Stafford Loan or an SLS (or your parents can get a PLUS for you while you're enrolled in the program).

Enrollment Deposit

Some colleges may require a deposit to reserve a space for the incoming student. Sometimes these deposits are required before you have received an acceptance notice or a financial aid package from other schools that you have applied to. If this is the case, send in the deposit and reserve your space. The worst thing that can happen is that you get better news that you've been accepted at a college which you would rather attend, or another college is offering you so much financial aid that you just can't say no. Either one of these is well worth losing your deposit over.

Entrance/Exit Interviews

Counseling sessions you must attend before you receive your first loan disbursement and again before you leave school (if you have any of the loans described in this book). At these sessions, your school will give you information on the full amount of your loan and its interest rate, the average amount borrowers owe, the amount of your monthly repayment, and information about deferment, refinancing, and loan consolidation options.

Equity Loan

A loan taken against the equity in your home (the excess of the market value of your home above your indebtedness).

Family Contribution Number (FC)

An amount, determined by a formula called the congressional formula, that indicates how much of your family's financial resources should be available to help pay for school. Factors such as taxable and non-taxable income, assets (such as savings and checking accounts or the value of a home), and benefits (for example, unemployment or social security) are all considered in this calculation. The FC is used in determining your eligibility for aid from the Supplemental Educational Opportunity Grant (SEOG), College Work-Study (CWS), Perkins Loan, and Stafford Loan programs. If you have any unusual expenses that may affect your family contribution, make sure you notify your financial aid administrator.

Important Note: Remember, your family contribution number is just a suggested amount given to the college by a *needs analysis service*. The actual amount of your family contribution is up to the financial aid administrator (FAA) at the college or university. They look over the entire picture and decide just how much financial aid you're going to get.

Federal Unsubsidized Stafford Loan

The new Stafford Loan program, available to all students regardless of financial need. This loan has the same low-interest rate and borrowing limits as the original Stafford Loan. However, the student must pay interest that accrues on the loan while the student is attending school.

Financial Aid

Money loaned or awarded the student by the federal and/or state governments, and the colleges themselves. Financial aid may consist of grants, loans, and/or work-study programs.

Financial Aid Administrator (FAA)

The FAA is the officer at an institution of higher education who is responsible for evaluating a student's eligibility for financial aid and decides the types and amounts of aid that will be awarded.

Financial Aid Analysis Services

Also known as needs analysis services, they are commercial enterprises that process your financial aid information and forward the results to colleges, the state, and back to you. The two most popular financial aid analysis services are the College Scholarship Service (CSS) and American College Testing (ACT).

Financial Aid Form (FAF)

A basic application for financial aid.

Financial Aid Package

The total amount of financial aid a student receives. Federal and non-federal aid such as grants, loans, or work-study are combined in a "package" to help meet the student's need. Using available resources to give each student the best possible package of aid is one of the major responsibilities of a school's financial aid administrator.

Financial Need (Eligibility)

The total cost of college per year, minus the family contribution number. Need serves as a basis for determining the amount of financial aid you will receive but does not guarantee that you will receive it.

Forbearance

A repayment option usually granted only under extenuating circumstances. It allows a student to hold off on the repayment of his or her student loans for a specified period of time.

Free Application for Federal Student Aid (FAFSA)

The application for federal student aid. Submission of this form is required in order to receive a financial aid award of any kind from the federal goverment. The FAFSA provides the basic information needed for determining a student's financial need. It is also the application for the Pell Grant.

General Education Development Certificate (GED)

A certificate students receive if they have passed a high school equivalency test. Students who don't have a high school diploma but who have a GED may still qualify for federal student aid. A school that admits students without a high school diploma must make available a GED program in the vicinity of the school and must inform students of the program.

Grade Point Average (GPA)

Sometimes financial grants from the colleges themselves are based upon the student maintaining a certain grade point average. The grade point average is a way of taking a student's marks and converting them into numbers:
(A=4 B+=3.5 B=3 C+=2.5 C=2 D=1 F=0)

If colleges give grants based on the maintenance of a 3.0 average, this means that the students must maintain a B average or they can kiss their grants good-bye.

Guarantee Agency

The organization that administers the Stafford Loan, PLUS, and SLS programs in your state. The federal government sets loan limits and interest rates, but each state is free to set its own additional limitations, within federal guidelines. This agency is the best source of information on Stafford, PLUS, and SLS loans in your state.

Half-time

At schools measuring progress by credit hours and academic terms (semesters, trimesters, or quarters), "half-time" means at least six semester hours or quarter hours per term. At schools measuring progress by credit hours but not using academic terms, "half-time" means at least 12 semester hours or 18 quarter hours per year. At schools measuring progress by clock hours, "half-time" means at least 12 hours per week. Note that schools may choose to set higher minimums than these. Also, Stafford Loan and PLUS requirements may be slightly different.

You must be attending school at least half-time to be eligible to receive a Pell Grant, Stafford Loan, or PLUS. Half-time enrollment is not a requirement to receive aid from the Supplemental Educational Opportunity Grant, College Work-Study, and Perkins Loan programs.

Home Equity

The monetary value of your home above the monetary value of any debt against it.

Home Value

The price you would get for your house if you were to sell it tomorrow, calculated using the Housing Index multiplier.

Housing Index

A government index used to derive a conservative estimate of the monetary value of your home. The derived value is based on the year in which your home was bought.

Income Protection Allowance

A predetermined amount of a family's income that will not be assessed by the congressional formula in the determination of a family's contribution number. The amount of income to be protected is determined by the size of the family household and the number of family members attending college at least half-time.

Independent Student

A student who is considered to be financially self-supporting. For automatic classification as an independent student, the student must meet at least one of the following:

the student must be at least 24 years of age

the student is a veteran of the U.S. armed forces

the student is a ward of the court or both parents are dead

the student has legal dependents other than a spouse

Students not claimed as dependents on their parent's tax returns for the last two years and students applying for financial aid may be considered for status as an independent student. The financial need of an independent student is based solely upon the student's own income and assets, without regard to the assets of his or her parents.

Interest

The amount of money above the principal that you must pay on a loan. Interest is compounded at regular intervals.

Internship Deferment

A period during which loan payments can be deferred (postponed) if a borrower is participating in an internship required by a state licensing agency to begin professional practice or service. An internship deferment is also given for participation in an internship or residency program leading to a degree or certificate awarded by an institution of higher education, a hospital, or a health care facility offering postgraduate training. For either type of deferment, the borrower's internship program must require the borrower to have a bachelor's degree before beginning the internship.

If you're in an eligible internship program, you may defer repayment of a Perkins Loan/NDSL or Stafford Loan for up to two years.

Note to Stafford borrowers: If you're in a *medical or dental* internship or residency program that exceeds two years, you will be granted forbearance for the remainder of your program. Although not a deferment, you may request forbearance if you're willing but unable to meet your repayment schedule and you're not eligible for a deferment. *Forbearance* means permitting payments to be stopped temporarily, allowing a longer time for making payments, or making smaller payments than were previously scheduled. You must submit a written request to the organization that holds your loan. That organization does not have to grant forbearance.

Legal Dependents

Persons for whom you are legally responsible for providing financial support, and whom you may claim as tax deductions when filing income tax returns.

Loan Consolidation

A plan that allows certain eligible lenders to pay off existing student loans and to create one new loan. You're eligible for loan consolidation if you have loans totalling at least $5,000. You must be in repayment (or have entered your grace period) before your loans can be consolidated. Repayment begins within 60 days after consolidation. The repayment period will be from 10 to 25 years, depending on the amount to be repaid. Except for PLUS Loans, the student loans described in this booklet are eligible for consolidation. Note that consolidation does not increase existing loan limits.

Need Blind Admissions

A policy by which the admissions decisions of a college are based entirely on the academic ability and character of the applicant, without regard to the applicant's ability or inability to pay for his or her education.

Needs Analysis Formula

The congressional formula used to determine your financial need and your family contribution number.

New Borrower

A term that applies to the Stafford, PLUS, or SLS Loan programs. You're a "new borrower" under these programs if, on the date you sign your *promissory note*, you have no outstanding (unpaid) balance on a Stafford, PLUS, or SLS made before July 1, 1987 for a period of enrollment beginning before July 1, 1987, and no outstanding balance on a consolidation loan made before July 1, 1987. Once you qualify as a new borrower, the loan conditions that apply to new borrowers automatically apply to any future Stafford or PLUS Loans you may receive.

Origination Fee

A charge for taking out a student loan, generally deducted from each loan disbursement made to you. The money goes to the federal government to help the costs of subsidizing low-interest loans.

Parental Leave Deferment

A period of up to six months when loan payments can be postponed if a borrower is pregnant, or if a borrower is taking care of a newborn or newly adopted child. The borrower must be unemployed and not attending school. To get this deferment, you must apply within six months after you leave school or drop below half-time status. (You must have been enrolled at least half-time while you were attending school.)

Parents' Contribution

This is the amount that a student's parents are expected to contribute towards their child's college education. This amount is calculated from age, income, assets, taxes, benefits, number of family members, and how many family members are attending college.

Pell Grant

A federal grant available only to very low-income students that does not have to be repaid. All students applying for financial aid must apply for a Pell Grant. The Pell Grant application serves as the basis for all financial aid judgments.

Pell Grant Index (PGI)

The number that appears on your Student Aid Report (SAR), telling you about your Pell Grant eligibility. The PGI is calculated by a standard formula that uses the financial information you reported when you applied for federal student aid.

Pension Plan

A plan providing for the disbursement of funds other than wages or salary, at regular intervals. Payments into the plan are tax deductible, and the principal may accumulate without taxes.

Perkins Loan

A low-interest student loan that is the sole responsibility of the student. Like the Stafford Loan, there is no accrual of interest while the student is in school. *This loan is made available only to first time college undergraduates*, and usually only those who have received a Pell Grant.

PLUS Loan (Parent's Loan to Undergraduate Students)

This is a low interest loan made to the *parents* of the student under more agreeable repayment terms than would otherwise be available. It is not considered by the author to be real financial aid.

Principal

The sum of money borrowed.

Promissory Note

The legal document you sign when you get a student loan. It lists the conditions under which you're borrowing and the terms under which you agree to pay back the loan. It's very important to *read and save* this document, because you'll need to refer to it later when you begin repaying your loan.

Refinancing

A loan repayment option whereby you resell your debt to the lender who then sets a new repayment agreement at a lower interest rate.

Refund Policy

The terms under which the college you are/will be attending will repay you for the educational expenses incurred in the event that you never register for classes or drop out shortly after classes start.

Regular Student

One who is enrolled in an institution to obtain a degree or certificate. Generally, to receive aid from the programs discussed in this booklet, you must be a regular student (For the Stafford, PLUS, and SLS Loan programs, there are two exceptions to this requirement. See the definition of *eligible program*).

Residency

Status granted by a state that will enable you to qualify for state financial aid and in-state tuition rates to state funded schools. Factors used in determining state residency are length of time in the state, employment and sources of financial support, payment of state taxes, and voting records.

Satisfactory Academic Progress

To be eligible to receive federal student aid, you must be maintaining satisfactory academic progress toward a degree or certificate. You must meet your school's written standard of satisfactory progress. Check with your school to find out what its standard is.

If you received federal student aid for the first time on or after July 1, 1987, and you're enrolled in a program that's longer than two years, the following definition of satisfactory progress also applies to you must be maintaining a C average by the end of your second academic year of study, or have an academic standing consistent with your institution's graduation requirements. You must continue to maintain satisfactory academic progress for the rest of your course of study.

Scholarship

A form of financial aid that is usually awarded to a student on a competetive basis due to a combination of merit, interest, and need. Scholarship money does not need to be paid back, but in the formation of a financial aid package it is deducted from your financial need rather than from your family contribution.

Scholarship Search Services

Usually commercial enterprises set up to locate scholarship money for eligible students.

SLS Loan

This program is the same as the PLUS Loan program, but instead of giving the loans to the parents, the SLS Loans are given to students who have been classified as independent.

Stafford Loan

A low-interest loan made to students enrolled at least half-time. *This loan can be taken out only by the student, and repayment is the student's responsibility.* There is no interest on the loan as long as the student is in school.

Statement of Educational Purpose

A statement that you must sign before you may receive federal financial aid. By signing this statement, you agree to use your financial aid award only for education-related expenses.

Statement of Registration Status

A statement that male applicants must sign in order to receive federal financial aid. This statement indicates whether or not you have registered with the Selective Service for call into the United States armed forces.

Student Aid Report (SAR)

The official notification of your financial aid eligibility. It contains information given on your application , your family contribution number, and confirms the list of colleges that your financial information has been sent to. It must be signed and submitted to the financial aid office of the school you will attend in order to receive payment of your financial aid award.

Student's Contribution

This is the amount of money a student is required to pay per year towards his or her college education. This amount is calculated from income, assets, social security, and any other benefits. It is the *student's contribution* plus the *parents' contribution* that become the *family contribution*.

Supplemental Educational Opportunity Grant (SEOG)

A federally funded government grant program that helps first time undergraduates with exceptional financial need. It is not a guaranteed grant, but is awarded based on the discretion of the FAA at the college to which you are applying.

Tax Deferred Annuity

With life insurance, it is one of two ways to shelter money so that it won't count against you when applying for financial aid. It is a payment made yearly to a savings plan, yielding high interest rates and tax deferred savings, yet is not assessed as an asset by the congressional formula.

U.S. Treasury Bill Rate

The basis of the interest rates for most student loans.

Validation

A process by which you must prove to the college that what you report on your FAF is correct. You will need to supply the college with copies of the student's and parents' income tax returns.

Veteran

Status granted to former members of the U.S. armed forces.

INDEX

ACKNOWLEDGMENTS

I'd like to thank Larry Freundlich of Freundlich Associates for his support, assistance, and ideas in the creation of this project and the editors and production staff at Council Oak Books for all of their help. Thanks also to my clients who have helped me prove that the college of their choice can be affordable no matter what their financial situations.

I would also like to thank my family: my wife Claudia and my son Adam for their support and confidence in me, my brother Martin and sister-in-law Lois for always being there when I needed them, my niece Michelle for her invaluable help, and especially Mom and Dad for inspiring me to do this important work.